MOUNTMELLICK
EMBROIDERY
edited by JULES & KAETHE KLIOT

This whitework embroidery technique is easily recognized by its bold ¹   s,
the natural floral motifs, the absence of any openwork, the ᵣ   ₑ
stitches, the typical fringed edges and the general overa"
ivory. Traditionally worked with heavy knitting cotton on
finished work was intended to be extremely durable and
Common projects were pillow shams, quilts, sachet cases an   ᴧ lınens.

A convent in the town of Mountmellick, Ireland, in the centeι ⌐ ιne textile industry, is
given credit for the origination of this technique in the early part of the 19th century.
Little has been written on this traditional Irish embroidery, which was a major factor in
the survival of the famine distressed Irish family in the mid 19th c. along with all other
varieties of handwork. In the latter part of the century the technique gained popularity
through the dissemination of patterns by the popular needlework magazines.

A finer variety of Mountmellick Embroidery is not unknown, using finer threads and
cotton fabrics. The rich variety of stitches can be used for embellishment on collars,
children's dresses and other general garments and linens.

WELDON'S PRACTICAL NEEDLEWORK, one of the more popular late 19th century
English needlework magazines presented, in series form, the most complete
instructions for executing this work, The complete set of 7 segments is presented in
this volume together with the Priscilla instructions which introduced Mountmellick to
the US audience in 1904.

CONTENTS:

Note: Numbers in [ ] designate page numbers of this book. Other page references are from original publications.

BIBLIOGRAPHY:

MOUNTMELLICK WORK, Jane Houston-Almqvist

SUPPLIES:

MOUNTMELLICK fabric, thread and other supplies available from:
LACIS, 2982 Adeline St., Berkeley, CA 94703

LACIS

PUBLICATIONS
3163 Adeline Street, Berkeley, CA 94703

© 1998, LACIS
ISBN 0-916896-94-3

WELDON'S PRACTICAL

MOUNTMELLICK EMBROIDERY

(FIRST SERIES.)

DESIGNS FOR THE VARIOUS STITCHES, BORDERS, AND FRINGES,

ALSO

GROUPED SPRAYS FOR DECORATIVE PURPOSES, AND NIGHTDRESS CASE.

SIXTY-TWO ILLUSTRATIONS.

MOUNTMELLICK EMBROIDERY.

MOUNTMELLICK EMBROIDERY is a handsome, strong, and durable work usually executed with Strutt's Knitting Cotton, in sizes varying from No. 6 to No. 14, on a ground of white satin jean; the embroidery is much raised, and is consequently thick and heavy, and requires a substantial material like jean to hold the stitches, for a foundation of thin texture would give way under the weight of the embroidery, but good firm materials being selected Mountmellick work will repay all the time and labour expended on it, as it is rich and effective in appearance, not difficult of execution when once the stitches are mastered, and moreover possesses the great merit of washing over and over again and remaining good to the last.

Mountmellick work is eminently suitable for quilts, pillow shams, toilet covers, nightdress sachets, comb and brush bags, and dressing-table mats and pincushions. Red ingrain cotton can be used if desired, but the real Irish Mellick work is always done with white, and nearly always keeping to one size of cotton throughout the piece of work. Strutt's No. 8 is a useful general size, or No. 6 and No. 10 may be employed together, the former for the running and padding of the flowers and leaves, and the latter for working over again in satin stitch, and for the numerous fancy stitches, some of which are peculiar to Mountmellick work, while others are common to various styles of embroidery. Use a crewel or other needle with an eye large enough to take the cotton easily.

Bold, handsome designs of flowers, such as passion flowers, sun flowers, lilies, &c., in groups, or in single flowers, are especially applicable to Mountmellick embroidery, and may be selected from Briggs' transfer patterns, and other sources, and ironed or traced upon the material in the usual manner. Small crowded designs will not show off the beauty of the work. Flowers are mostly worked in satin stitch highly raised, embellished with French knots and intermingled with fancy stitches, while leaves may be produced in flat or raised satin stitch, or with an outside row of French knots filled in with a veining

of feather stitch, or in other ways, and clusters of French knots represent berries, and likewise fill up the hearts of flowers.

All Mountmellick work is finished off with a row of buttonhole stitches round the outside margin, and completed with a knitted fringe.

Mountmellick work takes its name from a convent in Mountmellick, Ireland, where it originated, and it still is carried on extensively in that neighbourhood under the auspices of the Industrial Association, who make a *spécialité* of Mountmellick Embroidery in its modern form, with the object of assisting distressed Irish ladies and others by the sale of their work. The committee of this Association had the honour of presenting a beautifully worked toilet cover to the Princess of Wales on the occasion of Her Royal Highness's visit to Ireland in 1885.

A finer variety of Mountmellick embroidery is employed for pinafores and aprons, children's dresses and pelisses, and for the yokes and panels of ladies' costumes, for which holland, linen, sateen, and cashmere are appropriate materials, whereon the work would be carried out with embroidery cotton or flax thread on washing fabrics, and with knitting silk or embroidery silk on woollen goods; but in this form, though the Mountmellick stitches are employed and there must be no attempt at shading, the work bears a great resemblance to crewel work, and so loses its distinctive character.

No. 1.—Crewel or Outline Stitch, otherwise called Stem Stitch.

STITCHES USED IN MOUNTMELLICK EMBROIDERY.

No. 1.—Crewel Stitch, or Outline Stitch, otherwise called Stem Stitch.

This is identical with the stitch so much used in crewel work, and is employed for stems, and for veining up the centre of leaves, and frequently also for the outlining of leaves and flowers. To work, commence at the bottom of the stem or leaf and work upwards, bring the needle and cotton in front of the material, then insert the needle in the material in a slanting direc-

[3]

tion from right to left above the cotton and keeping the cotton to the right of the needle, draw through, take another stitch above in the same manner through only sufficient material to hold the stitch, and continue, making all the stitches the same size, not too closely together, and not drawing the cotton too tightly.

No. 2.—Overcasting.

A close firm stitch for stems. Work from left to right. Bring up the needle below the tracing line you are going to work upon, insert the needle above the tracing line and bring it out below in a direction slanting from right to left; every stitch is worked in the same manner, closely and regularly, side by side. This stitch may be varied to any width, and is sometimes slanted from left to right instead of from right to left; the appearance of the stitch is the same on the wrong side of the material as on the right.

No. 3.—Chain Stitch.

A very much used stitch, and requires to be done very regularly. Bring up the needle from the back of the material and draw up the cotton, hold the cotton down under the left-hand thumb and

and bring it up in a very slightly slanting direction one-eighth of an inch lower down and over the cotton held by the thumb, and draw up. If the stitches are taken quite closely together they appear linked something after the manner of chain stitch, but when worked further apart a light and branching effect is produced.

No. 5.—Snail-Trail Stitch.

This is much used in Mountmellick work for stems and outlining, where a very fine spotted tracery is desired; it may be done with the traced line you are going to work upon held straight toward you or from right to left. Bring up the cotton on the right side of the material on the traced line, hold the cotton under the thumb of the left hand, and passing the needle *over* the cotton held by the thumb insert it in the material on the left-hand side of the line about one-eighth of an inch from where it was before brought up and bring it up on the opposite side of the traced line, it thus passes below the material and below the cotton held by the thumb and over the cotton that is threaded in the needle, draw through, and by this process a long straight stitch and a small loop stitch will be formed, again hold the cotton under the thumb, and continue; the needle is set in only

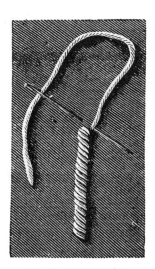

No 2.—Overcasting.

No. 3.—Chain Stitch.

No. 4.—Cording Stitch.

insert the needle in nearly the same place it came out, but just a thread or two to the right thereof, and bring it up about one-eighth of an inch lower down in quite a straight direction and over the cotton by the thumb, draw up; hold the cotton again under the left-hand thumb, insert the needle in the chain stitch just made, close to the right of where it has just been brought out, and bring the needle up one-eighth of an inch lower down in a straight direction and over the cotton held by the thumb, draw up, and repeat; and a series of loops like a crochet chain is formed on the right side of the material and a line of neat back stitches on the wrong side.

No. 4.—Cording Stitch.

An effective stitch for stems, for outlining leaves, and other purposes. Bring up the needle and cotton from the back of the material on the line to be embroidered, hold the cotton down under the thumb of the left hand, and insert the needle a little lower and a little to the right of the place it came out of, and bring it up one-eighth of an inch lower in a very slightly slanting direction and over the cotton held by the left-hand thumb, draw up; again hold the cotton under the thumb, insert the needle close by the place the cotton comes out of, but to the right outside the stitch just made,

a very slightly slanting direction upon the guiding line, as seen in engraving.

No. 6.—Cable Stitch.

This is a peculiar stitch, rather difficult to explain, but simple enough when understood, it is used chiefly for stems. Bring up the needle and cotton on the right side of the material, hold the cotton straight down under the thumb of the left hand, pass the needle from right to left under the cotton so held down, and draw it up till the cotton held under the thumb is brought to a small loop, then keeping the thumb in the same position insert the point of the needle in the material below the cotton and just underneath where you before brought it out, bring the point of the needle up in a straight line a quarter of an inch below, but *not* to pass through the loop of cotton that still is held under the thumb, release the thumb, and draw the loop of cotton closely round the top of the needle and pass the cotton from left to right under the point of the needle, as see illustration 6, and draw the needle at once through the little circular loop at top of the needle and through this present loop which resembles a chain stitch loop, and the stitch is accomplished; all the stitches are worked in the same manner, and the effect is as of a small knot of cotton linking one chain stitch to another. Be careful always to pull the cotton closely round the top of the needle and to loop it under the point of the needle as represented in the engraving before drawing the needle out, as if this is forgotten the stitch cannot be rightly formed, and it being a tiresome stitch to undo, great pains must be taken to work it correctly.

No. 7.—Double Cable Stitch.

This stitch is worked similarly to the preceding example, but instead of keeping it in a perfectly straight line take one stitch to the right and one stitch to the left alternately.

No. 8.—Cable Plait Stitch.

A highly ornamental stitch, closely twisted, and resembling a fancy plait; much used for stems, for outlining bold conventional designs, and various purposes. To work, trace two even parallel lines about a quarter of an inch distant the one from the other, and begin on the left-hand side to work from left to right,—bring up the needle and cotton on the lower tracing line, hold the cotton down under the left-hand thumb and pass the needle from right to left under the cotton so held and draw up till the cotton still held under the thumb

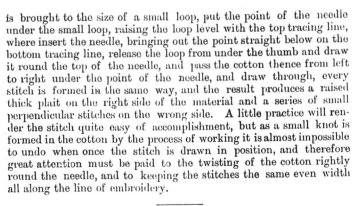

No. 5.—Snail-Trail Stitch

No. 6.—Cable Stitch.

is brought to the size of a small loop, put the point of the needle under the small loop, raising the loop level with the top tracing line, where insert the needle, bringing out the point straight below on the bottom tracing line, release the loop from under the thumb and draw it round the top of the point of the needle, and pass the cotton thence from left to right under the point of the needle, and draw through, every stitch is formed in the same way, and the result produces a raised thick plait on the right side of the material and a series of small perpendicular stitches on the wrong side. A little practice will render the stitch quite easy of accomplishment, but as a small knot is formed in the cotton by the process of working it is almost impossible to undo when once the stitch is drawn in position, and therefore great attention must be paid to the twisting of the cotton rightly round the needle, and to keeping the stitches the same even width all along the line of embroidery.

No. 9.—Cable Plait and Overcasting.

This is a pretty combination of the cable-plait stitch described above and the wide overcast stitch as in illustration 20; the cable-plait stitch is worked first, and then one stitch of the overcasting is added to each stitch of the plait, as seen in the engraving.

No. 10.—Single Coral Stitch.

The beauty of this stitch depends upon its perfect regularity, and a novice in working had better trace two perpendicular lines at a distance of about a quarter of an inch apart as a guide to ensure evenness. Having a needle threaded bring it up in the centre between the two lines, hold the cotton under the left-hand thumb and make a stitch quite straight on the line to the right bringing up the needle over the cotton held by the thumb, draw up; again hold the cotton under the thumb and now make a stitch straight on the line to the left, bringing up the needle over the cotton held by the thumb, see illustration 10; and continue thus working a stitch alternately on each side; the top of a new stitch must always be level with the bottom of the stitch last worked, and the cotton must not be drawn too tightly.

No. 11.—Double Coral Stitch.

This bears much resemblance to the preceding example, the only difference being that an additional stitch is made midway between the side stitches, as is clearly shown in the illustration.

No. 7.—Double Cable Stitch.

No. 8.—Cable Plait Stitch.

No. 12.—Single Feather Stitch.

A stitch that is effectively used in Mountmellick embroidery for the veining of leaves and for light open tracery. The great point is to work it quite evenly, which will require a little practice. Trace one perpendicular line on the material as a guide for the centre of the feather stitching, bring up the needle and cotton on this line, then hold the cotton under the left-hand thumb, insert the needle in a slanting direction on the right-hand side and taking up about one-eighth of an inch of material, bring it up the traced line just below the place it was before brought out and with the point of the needle over the cotton held by the thumb, draw through; again hold the cotton under the thumb, turn the needle completely round towards the left and take a similar stitch slanting to the centre and bringing the needle over the cotton held by the thumb, and draw through; again hold the cotton down and make a slanting stitch on the right-hand side, and hold the cotton down and make a slanting stitch on the left-hand side; and proceed thus, making the stitches radiate alternately right and left for the length desired.

No. 13.—Double Feather Stitch.

So called because *two* stitches are worked, one underneath the other, forming double branching lines on each side. The needle is always placed slanting in the material as detailed in the previous example. Double feather stitch is employed for small feathery sprays and grasses as well as for filling in leaves.

No. 14.—Treble Feather Stitch.

Another variety of this pretty stitch, by which three stitches are worked successively on each side.

No. 15.—Feather Stitch and Bullion.

In this example one side of the stem is worked in feather stitch as figure 12 and the other side in bullion stitch as illustration 16, which forms a very pretty combination. Or the two stitches can be otherwise varied by working one feather stitch and one bullion stitch alternately, the same on both sides; or by doing two feather stitches on each side, then a bullion stitch on each side, and so on; and other combinations will be suggested by the ingenuity of the worker.

No. 17.—Double Bullion Stitch.

A handsome stitch, rather more elaborate than the preceding, and consisting of two bullion stitches worked quite closely together, then a space, and two more bullion stitches, and so on, and corresponding pairs of stitches are worked on the opposite side of the central veining. This is the stitch used for working ears of barley, and occasionally for filling in the centres of flowers.

No. 18.—Herringbone Stitch.

This stitch is employed in flannel work to keep the hem down flat without making a double fold in the material, and it may be applied to the same purpose in embroidery, but is more often used as an ornamental stitch. When worked it resembles a series of small crosses which require to be formed with perfect regularity in even parallel lines. Trace two guiding lines on the material about a quarter of an inch apart from each other, or wider or narrower as the width of the herringbone is desired to be. Work from left to right. Bring up the needle on the right side of the material on the top line, insert the needle in the bottom line in a perfectly straight direction from right to left, taking up a few threads of the material and keeping the cotton to the right behind the needle, as in the engraving, draw through; take a stitch in the same manner on the

No. 10.—Single Coral Stitch.

No. 11.—Double Coral Stitch.

No. 9.—Cable Plait and Overcasting.

No. 12.—Single Feather Stitch.   No. 13.—Double Feather Stitch.   No. 14.—Treble Feather Stitch.

No. 16.—Bullion Stitch.

This stitch resembles a raised roll of twisted cotton lying on the surface of the material; it also is designated "roll picot stitch"; it is effectively employed to represent ears of corn and barley, for veining the centres of leaves, for working entire leaves (as illustration 29), and portions of flowers, and may be generally used whenever a raised ornamental stitch is desired. To work, bring up the needle and cotton to the front of the material, put the needle in the material in the position you wish the bullion stitch to lie, taking from a quarter of an inch to half an inch of material on the needle according to the length the stitch is required to be, and bring the point well out where the cotton already is, and with the needle standing in this position wind the cotton round the point of the needle ten or twelve times in the manner shown by illustration 29, wind the cotton with the right hand and keep the twist from falling off the needle by pressure of the left-hand thumb, then draw the needle through the material and through the twists of cotton, turn the cotton towards the top of the stitch and pull till the stitch lies in position with the twisted cotton in a close roll upon it, insert the needle again at the top of the bullion stitch and bring it up where the next bullion stitch is to begin. In the example, No. 16, the bullion stitches are worked as if branching right and left from a central veining which is done in crewel stitch after the bullion stitches are completed.

top line; and continue thus alternately, and the cotton of the last stitch forms a cross over the stitch preceding; take up the same amount of material on the needle to each stitch, and let the same space be left between the stitches, and draw the cotton just tight enough to lie smoothly, but not so tight as to pucker the material; and if working in a curved direction regulate the size of the stitches to the shape of the curve.

No. 19.—Wheat-Ear Stitch.

A pretty ornamental stitch, useful for grasses and sprays. To work, draw three perpendicular lines a quarter of an inch apart from each other, the centre line as a guide for the chain-stitch and the outer lines to regulate the size of the spikes. Bring up the needle on the centre line, hold the cotton under the left-hand thumb, insert the needle nearly in the same place as the cotton emerges from only a thread or two to the right, and bring it up on the same line a quarter of an inch lower down and over the cotton held by the thumb, draw through, this forms a chain stitch; insert the needle on the left-hand guiding line at the same level as you commenced the chain stitch and bring it out in the lower part of the chain stitch as represented in the engraving, draw through, insert the needle on the right-hand guiding line at the same level and bring it out again in the lower part of the chain stitch; next work another chain stitch, followed by a spike stitch on each side, and continue·

No. 20.—Wide Overcasting

This may be used for making an inside bordering upon the material within the line of buttonhole stitch with which Mountmellick worked articles are generally finished. The method of working overcasting has been already explained, see illustration 2. Leaves and small flowers and buds are frequently worked in overcasting, sometimes longitudinally and sometimes across and across from side to side, and when employed in this manner the stitch is identical with the well-known satin stitch.

No. 21.—Buttonhole Stitch.

Nearly all Mountmellick work is finished off with an outside bordering of buttonhole stitch, which may be straight and even, as in the present example, or jagged and indented as shown below. The stitch is worked similarly to the well-known buttonhole stitch used in English embroidery. Trace a guiding line to the size and shape the piece of material is to be cut to form the article you are working, and another line three-eighths of an inch or a quarter of an inch above to indicate the width of the stitches. It is a good plan to run a few darning stitches or couching threads to give solidity to the buttonhole edging. Work from left to right. Bring up the needle and cotton on the outside guiding line, press the cotton under the

graduated length, and a French knot is worked at the distance of a few threads above the longest stitch, the irregular length of the stitches of course pointing to the inside of the work.

No. 25.—Scolloped Buttonholing.

This is employed for toilet covers and other pieces of work. The tracing and buttonholing are executed in the manner already described, but the setting in of the stitches must be somewhat adapted to the shape of the scollop, as seen in the engraving.

No. 26.—Fringed Buttonholing.

This is a pretty variety of buttonholing to make use of when it is not intended to finish off the article with a knitted fringe. To work, bring up the needle on the outside guiding line, bring the cotton downwards and hold it under the left-hand thumb to the distance of half an inch or more, turn it up again, and insert the needle a quarter of an inch above where you just brought it out, but a trifle to the right, and take a stitch bringing up the needle on the line close to the right of where it was previously brought out, the cotton being to the right of the needle; make a taller stitch in the ordinary buttonhole way; * bring the cotton downwards and hold it

No. 15.—Feather Stitch & Bullion.   No. 16.—Bullion Stitch.   No. 17.—Double Bullion Stitch.

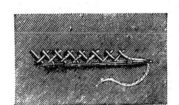

No. 18.—Herringbone Stitch.

No. 19.—Wheat-Ear Stitch.

thumb of the left hand, insert the needle in the upper guiding line and bring it up on the outside line and over the cotton held by the left-hand thumb, draw up, and continue, setting in the stitches closely together and all of equal height.

No. 22.—Saw-Tooth Buttonholing.

A very pretty effect is produced by working two tall and two short buttonhole stitches alternately, the spiky stitches appearing inside as a heading and the outer edge being quite straight.

No. 23.—Indented Buttonholing.

This has the appearance of small scollops, and is worked in sets of seven or more stitches of graduated length.

No. 24.—Buttonholing and French Knots.

The addition of French knots makes an elegant finish to the bordering of mats d'oyleys and other pieces of work; the bordering shown in our engraving is done in sets of five buttonhole stitches of

under the left-hand thumb to the distance of half an inch or more to form another loop of fringe, turn it up again, and insert the needle to take a taller stitch and bring out the needle close to the last stitch with the cotton to the right of the needle; make a still taller stitch in the ordinary buttonhole way; form another loop of fringe, and insert the needle to take a stitch at the same height as the one before the last and bring the needle out close to the last stitch with the cotton to the right of the needle; make a shorter stitch in the ordinary buttonhole way; then form another loop of fringe, and insert the needle to take a still shorter stitch (the same height as the stitch you commenced with) and bring the needle out close to the last stitch with the cotton to the right of the needle; make a taller stitch in the ordinary buttonhole way, and continue from *; take the stitches all as closely together as possible that the fringe may be thick, and you will have a regular series of indented buttonhole stitches combined with loops of fringe as in the engraving.

No. 27.—Couching.

As will be seen by our illustration, this consists of strands of cotton laid smoothly together and secured in place by stitches brought from the back of the material passing over the laid threads to the wrong side again. Couching is frequently used for large flowers, and occasionally for filling in certain designs where a solid horizontal, diagonal, or zigzag line is required. Stems are sometimes couched and consist of only one laid thread sewn over and over. The number of threads laid down may vary according as a more or less thick line is desired.

No. 28.—French Knots.

Knot stitch is effectively used in Mountmellick work to represent the seed vessels in the centre of flowers, for working the raised portions of various designs, such as berries, lilies, and others, and for

No. 20.—Wide Overcasting.

No. 21.—Buttonhole Stitch.

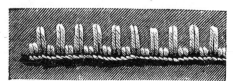

No. 22.—Saw-Tooth Buttonholing

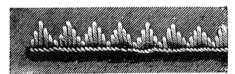

No. 23.—Indented Buttonholing.

retaining the cotton under the thumb of the left hand till ready to draw the knot to its proper degree of tightness. Larger French knots are made by twisting the needle four or five times round the cotton.

No. 29.—Bullion Stitch applied to a Leaf.

In our engraving this stitch is represented as if employed in working a leaf in place of satin stitch, for which purpose it is eminently useful; and very pretty leaves can be worked in the same manner but in two divisions, in the style of the leaf No. 38, the stitches being taken slantways towards the centre, and the indentation

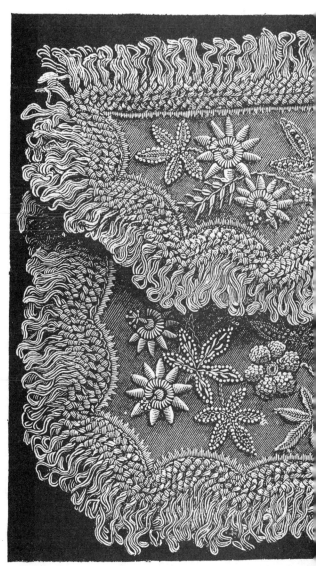

Nightdress Case in Mountmellick Work

a fancy outlining for certain flowers and leaves, for which last purpose the knots are produced in a row a little distance apart from each other along the traced outline, otherwise they are generally massed thickly together in a group. The mode of working is very simple. Bring up the needle and cotton on the right side of the material exactly where you desire the knot to be, hold the cotton under the thumb of the left hand and twist the needle twice round the cotton in the manner shown in the engraving, No. 28, then keeping the twist on the needle, turn the needle round and bring it gradually in an upright position and put it back in the material a thread or so behind where it came out, and with the point of the needle brought up in position for making the next knot, draw the needle through,

thereof forming of itself a veining up the middle of the leaf. In the example now under notice the stitches are taken across the leaf from side to side, and consequently vary in length, so that more twists of the cotton will be required to lay across the middle of the leaf than at the tip and the base. The method of working bullion stitch is explained by illustration and description No. 16.

No. 30.—Filling in. · Back Stitch.

So called because each stitch is taken backwards into the material beyond where the cotton was last drawn through, and the needle therefore passes along the back of the work and is brought up about two threads in advance, working from right to left ; the stitches should be small and regular, and set in closely together, following a straight or curved line according to the exigencies of the pattern. This is one of the simplest stitches used for filling in.

No. 31.—Filling in. Loop Stitch.

Also termed leaf stitch. When used for filling-in purposes this is worked in rows, leaving about a quarter of an inch of material between each loop, and the loops of the next row are arranged to come intermediately between the loops worked in the row preceding,

Design of Passion Flowers and Asters.

as shown in the engraving, No. 31. To work, bring up the cotton from the back to the right side of the material, hold the cotton under the left-hand thumb, and insert the needle in nearly the same place it came out of, only about a thread to the right, and bring it up about one-eighth of an inch lower down in a perfectly straight direction, the point of the needle passing over the cotton held by the thumb, draw up, insert the needle from the front to the back of the material below the loop stitch just made, and bring it up in proper position for making another loop stitch.

No. 32.—Filling in. Honeycomb Stitch.

This covers the surface of the material like a network, and is one of the prettiest stitches for filling in. Begin by drawing up the needle and cotton through the material at the left-hand top corner of the space to be filled in, insert the needle in the material one-eighth of an inch above the place you have just brought it out, and bring it up again to the same place as before, forming a simple perpendicular stitch, hold the cotton under the left-hand thumb, and about one-eighth of an inch to the right take another stitch similar to the last, bringing out the point of the needle over the cotton held by the thumb, like working a buttonhole stitch, and

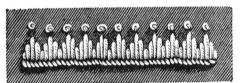

No. 24—Buttonholing and French Knots.

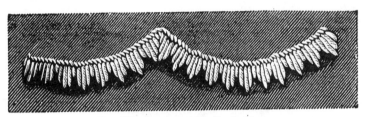

No. 25.—Scolloped Buttonholing.

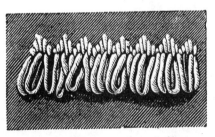

No. 26.—Fringed Buttonholing.

No. 28.—French Knots.

No. 27.—Couching.

proceed thus to the end of the space ; then work another buttonhole stitch row below this row, proceeding from right to left, making the stitches come intermediately between the stitches of last row, and inserting the needle above the horizontal threads of those stitches, and bringing it out one-eighth of an inch below and over the cotton held by the left-hand thumb ; and continue forwards and backwards in rows thus, till the filling in is completed.

No. 33.—Filling in. Brick Stitch.

There are two methods of working this stitch. By the first method you proceed in a manner similar to honeycomb, but taking shorter stitches and working them farther apart, so that there is a greater space of material between the stitches. The other method is to couch the heavy lines with two or three strands of cotton laid upon the material, and kept in place by bringing up a stitch from the back of the material, passing over the strands and returning again to the back, and afterwards making stitches from couching to couching at equal distances apart, and so arranging that one stitch comes midway between two stitches of last row, in the manner shown in the illustration, No. 33.

No. 34.—Filling in. Diamond Pattern.

A very effective stitch for filling in large spaces, and very quickly done. First of all, carry long vertical stitches across the space to be filled in, going first from top to bottom and then back from bottom to top, or otherwise from side to side, as may be most

opposite direction, and forming a diamond network. Wherever the threads cross each other work over them a simple cross stitch, as illustration 35, this ornaments the leaf, and at the same time serves to keep in place the threads of the diamond crossing. This is an extremely pretty background stitch, and may frequently be employed for filling large spaces with good effect.

No. 36.—Margin of a Leaf worked in Outline Stitch.

This consists merely of working over the traced margin of a leaf with a line or two of crewel or outline stitch, or simple overcast stitch, taking short slanting stitches all along to cover the tracing effectually; the stitches slant downwards from the outside towards the centre of the leaf, both sides alike.

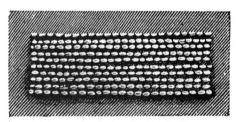

No. 30.—Filling in. Back Stitch.

No. 29.—Bullion Stitch applied to a Leaf.

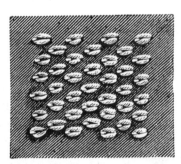

No. 31.—Filling in. Loop Stitch.

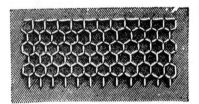

No. 32.—Filling in. Honeycomb Stitch.

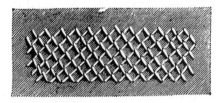

No. 34.—Filling in. Diamond Pattern.

No. 33.—Filling in. Brick Stitch.

No. 36.—Margin of a Leaf worked in Outline Stitch.

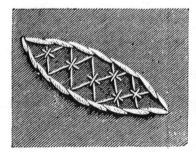

No. 35.—Filling in a Leaf. Diamond Stitch and Cross Stitch.

convenient, but always in the same direction, and in such a way that the cotton nearly all passes upon the surface of the material; then to cross, pass the needle from right to left under the thread of cotton nearest to the left hand, then from right to left under the next thread of cotton, and so on, keeping the cotton you are working with always below the needle, and when you get to the opposite side insert the needle to the back of the material and bring it up again ready for the next crossing, which work reversely, at such a distance from the first as will produce nicely shaped diamond meshes.

No. 35.—Filling in a Leaf. Diamond Stitch and Cross Stitch.

Work the outline of the leaf in the usual manner. Then take long stitches across the leaf from side to side in a slanting direction; and work again in long slanting stitches, crossing the first in the

No. 37.—Method of working a Leaf in Flake Stitch.

Flake stitch is a variety of satin stitch employed for rather large leaves whereby the design is filled in with stitches of unequal length, mixing invisibly, and altogether forming a smooth even surface; the mode of working is clearly shown in the illustration, where a little space has been purposely left between each stitch to render the detail more explicit, but in actual work the stitches seem as if blended one into the other in a continuous whole. The outer row of flake stitches is worked first, doing one long stitch and one short stitch alternately; then in the second row fill the spaces carrying the stitch longer than the stitches of the first row, and do a short stitch alternately; and in the third row fill in the spaces left in the second row and carry these stitches longer than the previous ones, and so on to the centre line that must be observed for the vein of the leaf. If there is any ridgy appearance it will look bad, therefore be careful to work very smoothly.

No. 38.—A Leaf worked in Flat Satin Stitch or Overcast Stitch.

This is a very favourite stitch for leaves by which the entire surface is worked over and over in two divisions from the outside slanting to the centre, the double line of stitches forming a kind of vein down the centre of the leaf. Trace the outline and also the centre line. The stitches are taken closely together side by side, all perfectly flat and regular, and all slanting in the same direction, not a space of material should be visible between the stitches, and as in satin stitch the same as in overcasting the needle passes along the back of the material, the leaf presents much the same appearance at the back of the work as upon the surface. Leaves with an indented outline, such as rose leaves, look well worked in this manner.

No. 39.—A Leaf worked in Raised Satin Stitch.

When a raised effect is desired in flowers and leaves it is generally produced by darning threads of coarse cotton, more or less thickly, within the outline. This darning must lie as much as possible upon

the needle in the tip of the leaf and bring it out where the cotton already is, and draw through; hold the cotton under the left-hand thumb, insert the needle in the outline on the right-hand side of the leaf, close by the last stitch, bringing it out in the centre vein over the cotton held by the thumb, and draw through, hold the cotton again under the thumb, insert the needle in the outline on the left-hand side of the leaf, and bring it out in the centre vein over the cotton held by the thumb, and draw through, and proceed, doing alternately a stitch to the right and a stitch to the left, always quite close to the preceding stitch. The length of the stitches will vary to give an intended appearance to the outside of the leaf, and the mode of working feather stitch produces a pretty plait to simulate a central vein.

No. 41.—A Leaf worked in Trellis Stitch.

Hold the material so as to proceed from right to left, and begin by bringing out the needle at the tip of the leaf; hold the cotton under the left-hand thumb, and take a stitch from right to left on

No. 38.—A Leaf worked in Flat Satin Stitch.

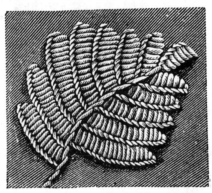

No. 42.—A Large Leaf worked in Buttonhole Stitch.

No. 39.—A Leaf worked in Raised Satin Stitch.

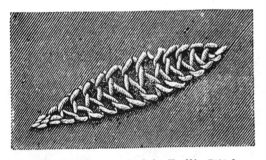

No. 41.—A Leaf worked in Trellis Stitch.

No. 37.—Method of working a Leaf in Flake Stitch.

No. 40.—A Leaf with Serrated Edge worked in Feather Stitch.

the surface of the material, that is, only taking on the needle sufficient material to hold the stitch, and it must always run in the contrary direction from that in which the leaf is to be worked, as in example No. 39, the darning threads or padding pass from the top to the bottom of the leaf in two divisions, and are thick and solid in the centre of each division, and graduate down on both sides, while the satin stitch is worked from the outside to the centre, the same as in the preceding example. But as this method occupies a great deal of time it is advisable in the case of working large and highly-raised designs to pad with a piece or two of cotton wool, which is fastened in place with a few cross stitches, and then worked once over and finally finished with satin stitch.

No. 40.—A Leaf with Serrated Edge worked in Feather Stitch.

Trace upon the material the outer margin of a leaf with a line for the centre vein. Bring the needle and cotton up on the right side of the material on the centre vein nearly at the tip of the leaf, insert

the lower outline below the thread held by the thumb, and so that the point of the needle passes over the cotton, draw through, hold the cotton again under the left-hand thumb, and take a stitch on the top outline passing the cotton from under the thumb to go under the point of the needle, draw through, and repeat these two motions, taking the stitches close together upon the outline, widening the trellis to the shape of the leaf and gradually narrowing as you approach the end (see illustration 41). The leaf may, or may not, be outlined round the outside of the trellis stitch, according to taste. A pretty twisted appearance can be given to this stitch by passing the needle from left to right under the cotton on the completion of each stitch.

No. 42.—A Large Leaf worked in Buttonhole Stitch.

Our engraving represents a fern leaf worked in rows of simple Buttonhole Stitch. Do not break off the cotton at the end of a line, but turn and work the next line backwards, and so go on working forwards and backwards till one half of the leaf is completed, when work the other half to correspond. A veining of outline stitch is afterwards worked up the centre of the leaf.

No. 43.—Method of working a Simple Flower.

The simple flower shown in our engraving is worked in slightly raised satin stitch, the satin stitches being taken over and over from side to side. Proceed thus,—First of all trace the design upon the material, then run a thread of cotton round each of the five petals of the flower, and fill them in with a darning of stitches taken lengthways to form a foundation or padding for the satin stitch; begin the satin stitch at the tip of a petal and work across from side to

No. 43.—Method of work-
ing a Simple Flower.

No. 44.—Pansy Flower in Buttonhole Stitch
and Honeycomb.

No. 46.—Spider Web   No. 47.—Loop Stitch   No. 48.—Cog Wheel
Ring.   Ring   Ring.

side closely and smoothly, shaping the stitches in accordance with the outline, wider in the centre of the petal, and gradually narrowing as the base is approached, and when all five petals are completed, fill up the centre of the flower with a cluster of six French knots to represent seed vessels. Sometimes this method is reversed, and the padding is darned across the petals, and the satin stitch is worked longitudinally; or, if a flat appearance is desired, work simply satin stitch without any padding whatever.

No. 44.—Pansy Flower.

This flower consists of five petals all outlined with buttonhole stitch a quarter of an inch deep, and the centres of the petals are filled in

with honeycomb. The stem is cording stitch. All these stitches have been already explained, and the method of combining them will easily be seen by a study of the illustration.

No. 45.—Leaf Stitch as used for a Small Spray.

Leaf Stitch is worked thus,—Bring the needle up on the line of stem where a leaf is to be worked, hold the cotton under the left-hand thumb, and insert the needle in the place it came out of and take up about a quarter of an inch of material and bring it out over the cotton held by the thumb, and draw through, put the needle to the back of the work over the top of the leaf; continue thus making tiny leaves on each side the line of stem, and after forming a leaf at the tip of the stem work down the stem in outline stitch; do the

No. 49.—Knitted Fringe for Trimming Mountmellick Work.

No. 45.—Leaf Stitch as used for a Small Spray.

other portions of spray in the same manner: the thicker part of the stem downwards from where the sprays meet is worked in snail-trail stitch.

No. 46.—Spider-Web Ring.

Begin in the centre of the ring, and work outline stitch round and round for the size required. Rings are occasionally used for filling in vacant spaces.

No. 47.—Loop-Stitch Ring.

This is a circle of twelve loops worked in the same manner as the loop stitch illustrated by No. 31. Bring the needle up where the centre of the ring is to be, hold the cotton down below the thumb of the left hand, and take a long stitch from the centre (where the cotton is brought out) to the outside of the intended circle, bringing the needle up through the loop of cotton held by the thumb as if working a chain stitch, draw the cotton to the size the loop is required, and insert the needle to the back of the work over the tip of the loop stitch, and continue, regulating the diameter of the circle so as to get twelve loop stitches at equal divisions round the ring.

No. 48.—Cog-Wheel Ring.

This consists of twelve roll picots, or bullion stitches, in the circle; for the manner of working these stitches see illustration 16.

Spray of Honeysuckle.

No. 49.—Knitted Fringe for Trimming Mountmellick Work.

Wind a supply of No. 12 knitting cotton upon four separate balls and use from all four balls together, working with a pair of No. 11 steel knitting needles. Cast on 12 stitches. **1st row**—Make 1 (by passing all four strands of cotton round the needle), knit 2 together, knit 1, and repeat this three times. Every row is the same. When you have knitted a sufficient length to go nicely round the article you intend trimming, cast off 7 stitches, break off the cotton, and draw the end through the last stitch on the right-hand needle. Slip the 5 remaining stitches off the left-hand needle, and unravel them all the way along, and a pretty crinkled fringe will be produced. Sew the fringe by the loop stitches that are at the top of the heading to the edge of the buttonhole stitches that border the piece of Mountmellick embroidery.

SPRAY OF HONEYSUCKLE.

THE honeysuckle flowers are of French knots placed thickly together, and with the stamens worked in back-stitch with a very small French knot on the tip of each stamen. The stem is worked throughout in cording stitch; and the leaves are executed in satin stitch across from side to side, raised over a darned or padded foundation, excepting one or two of the leaves at the top of the stems which are in simple flat satin stitch.

SPRAY OF BLACKBERRIES, FLOWERS, AND LEAVES.

THE blackberries are composed of clusters of French knots worked closely together, and with rather large knots made in the centres of the berries to produce a kind of spherical appearance. The flowers are embroidered in raised satin stitch worked lengthways over a darned or padded foundation; there are five petals in each flower, with a group of three small French knots in the centre. The lower portion of the stem is worked in cable-plait stitch, on each side of which here and there a spike stitch is put to simulate a thorn, the remainder of the stem being carried out in crewel stitch, cording stitch, and snail-trail stitch. One large leaf is executed in feather stitch, alternating from side to side to the centre where the crossing

Blackberry Flowers, Berries, and Leaves.

of the cotton produces a natural vein; and the other leaf is delineated with an outline of French knots, and filled in with a veining of crewel stitch and bullion stitches.

NIGHTDRESS SACHET.

PROCURE a piece of white satin jean material, 26 inches long by 17 inches wide, and from this cut a 10½-inch length for the front of the Nightdress Sachet, leaving a 15½-inch length to form the back and to turn over for the flap. Use Strutt's best Knitting Cotton, No. 12, for the Mountmellick embroidery. Trace the design upon the front of the sachet, and on the flap, as shown in the engraving, and proceed to work the passion flowers, executing the sepals in raised Satin stitch, the arc in Bullion stitch, and the centres as delineated,—in some of the flowers a centre of Satin stitch, and stamens simulated by Backstitching and French knots, in others a ray of five or six long stitches, with a French knot on the tip of each stitch. The campanula flowers are worked in French knots, very thickly raised, six petals form a flower, and the disc is filled in with a tiny circle of Buttonhole stitches. Some of the leaves are embroidered with a

Branch of Hops.

margin of French knots, and filled inside with Trellis stitch, elongated to shape; others are similarly outlined with French knots, and veined with Crewel stitch and Bullion stitch, while others are buttonhole-stitched in outline, and filled in with one central line of French knots up each segment of the leaf; and others, again, are worked in Feather stitch, the twist of the stitch itself forming a line of veining down the centre of the leaf. The ears of barley are embroidered in Double-Bullion stitch, with a Spike stitch added on the point of each ear. The stems are in Crewel stitch and Cording stitch, and the tendrils are Snail-trail stitch. When the Mountmellick embroidery is all completed, the front piece of the Nightdress Sachet is turned down in a narrow hem where the sachet opens. Then the material is buttonhole-stitched together in scollops, and the same buttonholing carried round the flap, as represented in our illustration, and a straight line of indented buttonholing is worked along the fold at the top of the flap. Cut away the surplus material from the outside of the scollops, and trim the sachet with fringe, knitted according to the directions for No. 49, but only casting on 9 stitches, and when a sufficient length is done to go round the sachet cast off 5 stitches, draw the cotton through the stitch on the right-hand needle, and unravel the remaining 3 stitches for fringe.

BRANCH OF HOPS.

THE flowering spray of hops is worked entirely in Satin stitch, which is fully described and illustrated on page 11; the large leaf is outlined with French knots, as illustrated on page 9, and described on page 8, and filled in with Crewel stitch and Bullion stitches, so clearly illustrated by No. 16, on page 7, while the description for same appears on page 6; and the small leaf is worked in Feather stitch after the manner of the leaf, figure 40, while the stem is successfully delineated in Snail-trail stitch, for which refer to illustration 5 on page 5, while it is described on previous page. It is as effective a design as any one could wish for, and not difficult to work, while the variety of stitches needed for its execution render it attractive and uncommon.

SPRAY OF FERN.

NOTHING prettier or more natural could be desired than this spray of fern leaves, which would form a pretty centre piece to a d'oyley, or corners to a larger piece of work, while a series of these sprays could be nicely transformed into a running border. The stem is worked throughout in Cording stitch, so clearly illustrated on page 4, by illustration 4. The leaves are composed of Satin stitch, worked after the style shown by illustration 38, and which must be done as smoothly and evenly as possible, and worked from outside to the centre; some of the stitches are longer than others to mark

Spray of Fern

indentations of the leaves. However, our illustration so clearly defines every stitch that little difficulty will be experienced in copying this graceful design.

BESIDES the designs given, ladies will find mountain ash berries and leaves, or acorns and leaves very effective in Mountmellick work, while vines and grapes, wheat, barley, pomegranates, iris, lilies, &c., are also very suitable, it being necessary to choose bold handsome designs, while the various stitches given in this issue are equal to all demands, and will serve to execute from the most simple to the most elaborate piece of work. For toilet covers or mats, bed spreads and such articles, Mountmellick work is without equal for beauty of design and durability.

WELDON'S PRACTICAL
MOUNTMELLICK EMBROIDERY

(SECOND SERIES.)

New and Original Designs for Toilet Covers, Mats, Brush and Comb Bags;

ALSO

Artistic Grouped Sprays for Decorative Purposes.

TWENTY ILLUSTRATIONS.

MOUNTMELLICK EMBROIDERY.

In our first issue on Mountmellick Embroidery, which forms No. 45 of "Weldon's Practical Needlework Series," we illustrated and explained the method of executing the stitches employed in this favourite work, and we now supply our readers with a variety of new and handsome designs originated expressly for this series, and intended to show the application of the various stitches to the practical working of leaves, flowers, &c., from the most simple spray to a large and elaborate piece of work. Our engravings represent as clearly as possible the exact working of each subject, and are so well defined that further explanation is almost unnecessary to any one who has carefully studied and worked out the numerous examples in our previous issue. However, to simplify matters to even the most inexperienced worker, a detailed description is given with each design explanatory of the stitches used and the manner of successfully combining them, and reference is constantly made to the examples in No. 45 of "Weldon's Practical Needlework Series," where the different stitches are shown separately and in full working size.

As a rule, certain stitches are used for certain subjects because they have been found so to produce the best effect, but there is great scope left for originality, and if really tasteful combinations of stitches are arranged in a pleasing way, in an artistic design, the effect cannot fail to be satisfactory. One thing to be observed, the stitches, especially the raised satin stitches and the padding thereof, must be of proper consistency, neither too loose nor too tight, for if too tight they will pucker and contract the material, and though steaming and careful ironing can modify this to a certain extent, it can never restore the fabric entirely to its pristine smoothness; on the other hand, if the stitches are too loose, the work has an unskilful. slovenly appearance, and the cotton is apt to be drawn out of place. Great care then must be taken to work with exactness, and experience will determine the happy medium. The best quality of white satin jean should be employed for the foundation, and the work should be done with Strutt's knitting cotton, the

Spray of Campanula, Blossoms and Leaves.

cotton put up in yellow packets with a pink tie is the best quality, and No. 8 is a good useful size.

A great deal of highly raised work is introduced into the best specimens of Mountmellick embroidery, and certainly conduces greatly to the beauty of the work. "Raising the design" is simply covering that portion of the design with cotton in order to *raise* the embroidery above the surface of the fabric; very rich and natural

Pansy Spray.

effects are produced in this way. In order to accomplish the purpose you go inside the outline with an ordinary darning stitch, just as you would darn a stocking, and continue taking stitches backwards and forwards, across and across, until the whole surface of that part of the design you wish raised is covered; sometimes the greater part of the darning is piled well up in the centre, sometimes it is more to the right than the left, or *vice versâ*, but either way take care to preserve the form and character of the design, and work satin stitch smoothly and evenly at the top of all.

The rounding of corners and sharp turns in working various designs requires that the stitches should be taken in a skilful manner to preserve the same uniform direction: as, for instance, the needle must be inserted at a right angle at the top of leaves to ensure the proper slope preparatory to working down the other side. When working buttonhole stitch in a circle to form the eye of a flower, always on the completion of the circle avoid showing a join, by passing the needle under the loop of the first stitch to the back of the material. When doing scolloped buttonholing be careful to bring the corners of the scollops neatly together. Fasten on the cotton by a few running stitches, never with a knot, and finish off by drawing it through some part of the work that is already finished. Many other small "neatnesses" will occur as one gets accustomed to the style of the embroidery.

To "conventionalize a flower" is to convert its real shape and habit into a purely ornamental design, and this is nearly always done in adapting natural subjects to decorative needlework; the principal flowers are placed where they will show to the best advantage, and buds, leaves, and other accessories are arranged to fill in the available space with the object of producing the best and most natural effect.

Many ladies are skilful in sketching their own designs from Nature and applying the same in a clever manner to the purpose in hand The most effective designs for Mountmellick embroidery are those

composed of rather large flowers, as the subjects must be bold to work out well. A good selection of subjects will be found on subsequent pages, and also examples of several handsome fully worked articles.

Designs may be enlarged or contracted by means of a pantograph, an instrument that is procurable for a trifle at any establishment where artists' materials are sold. Another way of enlarging a design is to draw a series of small squares over the example, and a series of the same number of larger squares on a sheet of paper the size the design is required to be, then follow square by square the intricacies of the pattern, crossing a line where the line is crossed in the original, and keeping to the general outline until the design completed.

Designs can be traced upon the material by the aid of carbonic paper—lay the paper face downwards upon the material and on it place the design, steadying both in position by a weight or two, then carefully go over the whole of the design with the blunt point of a crochet needle, and on removing the carbonic paper the pattern will be found clearly marked upon the fabric, but be careful not to press either of your hands heavily on any part while you are tracing or an undesirable impression may be left. The same piece of carbonic paper will serve for tracing many designs. This method of tracing has quite superseded the old way of rubbing pounce through holes pricked along the outline of the design.

Mountmellick work should be washed in lukewarm soapy water, rinsed in clear water, and dried quickly, but while still a little damp, stretch it carefully and lay it right side downwards on a clean cloth spread over an ironing blanket folded four or five times, and iron it with a moderately warm iron till quite dry.

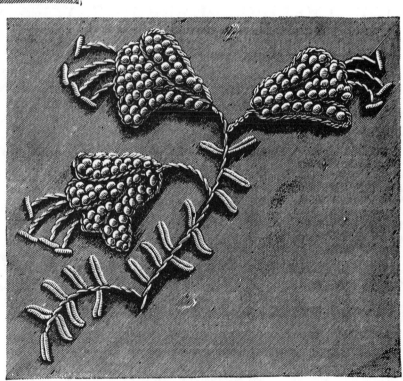

Spray of Bell-shaped Lilies.

SPRAY OF CAMPANULA, BLOSSOMS AND LEAVES.

This is as handsome a design as any one could wish for, and not difficult to work. It may be used as a running border, or be arranged in a set design for a sideboard cloth, toilet cover, and other purposes. The star-like flower of the campanula is extremely pretty, and is most effectively rendered in satin stitch worked across from side to side of the petals over a thickly padded foundation or darning which is first of all run in lengthways to afford substance sufficient to raise the flowers well above the surface of the material; there are six petals radiating from a centre composed of three small French knots, as will be clearly seen on reference to the engraving, while French knots are illustrated on page 9, and described on page 8, in No. 45 of "Weldon's Practical Needlework Series." The stem is worked in chain stitch, and the tendril in snail trail stitch, both of which are illustrated and fully described in No. 45 of this series and which is entirely devoted to Mountmellick work. The leaves,

with flake stitch, the other three petals being outlined with snail trail stitch with a few thick satin stitches worked at the extreme top, and three or four darts of crewel stitch filling in the centre. The buds are outlined with overcast stitch, the base being raised satin stitch from which spring three bullion stitches. The stem is worked in cable stitch throughout. The seven largest leaves are executed in buttonhole stitch worked from the centre to the margin, some stitches being longer than others to define the correct shaping of the leaf; a mid rib of crewel stitch forms the veining. The two small leaves at the lower part of the spray are worked in bullion

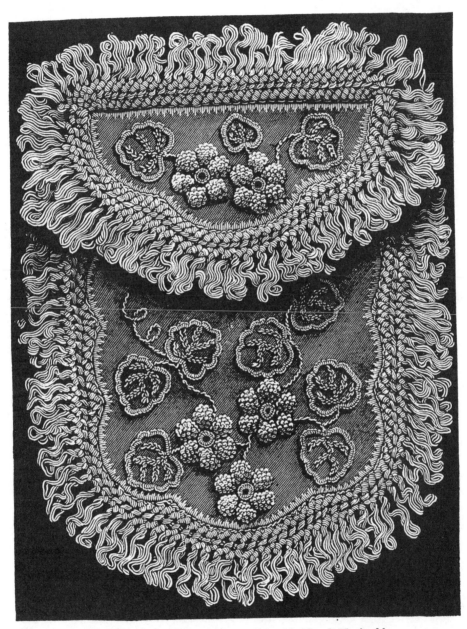

Brush and Comb Bag. Design of Double Marsh Marigolds.

which are long and slightly serrated, are outlined in French knots, and filled in with a veining of coral stitch in some leaves and feather stitch in others.

———

PANSY SPRAY.

THE pansy flower represented in our engraving will form a pretty subject for the centre of a d'oyley and other purposes, or it may be nicely transformed into a running border. The method of working the flower is as follows,—The two upper petals are filled in entirely

stitch, exactly as the example of bullion stitches in Nos. 16 and 17, page 7, No. 45 of "Weldon's Practical Needlework Series," where will also be found an explanation of all the other stitches mentioned in the working of this flower.

———

SPRAY OF BELL-SHAPED LILIES.

THESE lilies are of smaller size than the white lilies illustrated in the previous example; they however make a very pretty spray, and may with advantage be worked in a group by themselves or mixed with other flowers according to taste and the purpose for which the design is intended. Each petal of the lily flower is outlined with snail trail stitch, within which large French knots are thickly introduced; the stamens worked in crewel stitch are rather short, and an anther composed of one small bullion stitch is attached to the tips of each stamen, as shown in the engraving. The stem is worked in crewel stitch, and the small leaves which branch out at intervals on each side the stem are delineated by working rather long bullion stitches quite closely together in pairs.

BRUSH AND COMB BAG.

DESIGN OF DOUBLE MARSH MARIGOLDS.

For this useful bag procure two pieces of white satin jean, one piece 11 inches long by 8½ inches wide for the front of the bag, and

1st row—Make 1 (by passing all four strands of cotton round the needle), knit two stitches together, knit 1, repeat this twice. Every row is the same. When a sufficient length is knitted, cast off 5 stitches, draw the cotton through the stitch on the right-hand needle, breaking off the cotton and unravel the remaining 3 stitches for fringe. Sew the fringe by the loop stitches at the top of the heading to the edge of the buttonhole stitches that border the piece of needlework. A nightdress sachet should be made to match the brush and comb bag; while there is a charming design for a nightdress case on page 8 of No. 45 of "Weldon's Practical Needlework Series."

TOILET MAT.

SHELL OF THE FORAMINIFERA SPECIES.

The shell in the accompanying design is an exceedingly handsome

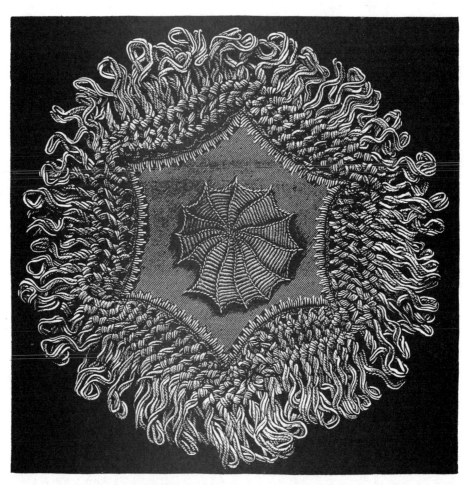

Toilet Mat. Shell of the Foraminifera Species.

the other piece 16 inches long by 8½ inches wide to serve for the back and the flap, which are in one, and of this only the flap is worked. The embroidery is executed with Strutt's best knitting cotton, No. 8. Trace out the design of double Marsh Marigolds, as shown in the illustration, and work it in accordance with the instructions given on page 12 for the working of a similar design. When the embroidery is thus accomplished you have to work a line of scolloped buttonholing all round the material except on the short side at the top of the front, which is simply turned down and hemmed. Do a line of straight buttonhole stitch at the top of the flap where it turns over. Make up the bag, and trim it all round with pretty knitted fringe, as in the engraving. The method of knitting this fringe is as follows: Wind a supply of knitting cotton upon four separate balls and use from all four balls together, working with a pair of No. 10 or No. 11 steel knitting needles. Cast on 9 stitches.

subject. It is composed of thirteen sections, each section being embroidered with rows of bullion stitches extending across from side to side; very small stitches with the cotton wound only twice or three times round the needle are used in the centre of the shell, and they gradually increase in length, till as the outside margin is approached they are brought to a termination in points or angles; the indentations between the sections are marked out by lines of crewel stitch, and an edge of crewel stitch extends round the outside of the shell like a couching. The mat is finished to correspond with the mat described on page 7.

SMALL MAT.

CLUSTER OF STRAWBERRIES AND FERN LEAVES.

THESE small mats are very useful either for the dressing table or as dessert d'oyleys. A dozen may be worked each in a different design and would sell quickly at bazaars or be very acceptable as a present. The design of strawberries and fern leaves selected for our engraving is especially pretty and effective. The material used is white satin jean, and the embroidery is done with Strutt's knitting cotton, No. 10. The strawberries are slightly raised and worked in flake stitch, lengthways, with here and there a tiny French knot dotted about to represent the seeds seen in the natural fruit. The unripe berry at the top of the stem is worked in flat satin stitch, and the calyx to this as well as the calyx to the ripe fruit is depicted by overcast stitching. The two fern leaves are executed in buttonhole stitch in branching lines, with a mid rib worked in crewel stitch. The mat is six-sided, each side being curved inwards in the work Series," which is the 1st issue on Mountmellick embroidery, showing all the elementary stitches and necessary details, and the Toilet Mat of Wild Roses, on page 11 of the present number, where these subjects impart a pleasing lightness and variety to the more solid portion of the work, and are valuable aids in bringing the designs to a satisfactory conclusion. Grass may be advantageously combined with almost any flowers, but wheat and barley are appropriate only to be mingled with wild flowers or with garden flowers, that bloom in the autumn of the year, such as dahlias, sunflowers, poppies, &c., and would of course be incongruous in combination with lilies, forget-me-nots, or other spring blooming or early summer flowers. Grains of wheat are invariably represented by bullion stitches, executed in the manner illustrated No. 16, page 7, of No. 45 of "Weldon's Practical Needlework Series," and a spike stitch or two outline stitches are worked on the top of each bullion stitch to simulate the beard; the ears of barley being thicker than wheat are depicted by double bullion stitches, and completed with a

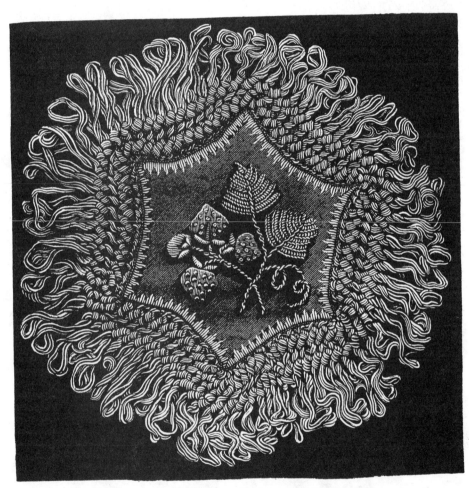

Small Mat. Cluster of Strawberries and Fern Leaves.

form of a scollop, and the six scollops, or sides, are defined by indented buttonholing, and the mat is finished off with a pretty bordering of knitted fringe, instructions for knitting which are appended to the description of the Brush and Comb Bag, page 6.

WHEAT, BARLEY, AND GRASS.

OUR engraving represents an ear of wheat, a stalk of barley, and two blades of grass, grouped together in an easy and natural manner, so as to form a pretty subject for the centre of a small d'oyley. The mode of working each is clearly visible. Wheat, barley, and grass are often introduced into a large design to fill up spaces where it would not be advisable to overload the pattern with additional flowers and leaves; see the nightdress case of passion flowers and asters on pages 8-9, No. 45 of "Weldon's Practical Needle-

spike stitch to every pair of bullion stitches; the stem in both instances being of simple outline or crewel stitch. Blades of grass are successfully imitated by simple overcast stitch following upon the tracing of the design in stitches slanting from side to side. In short, the subjects of this engraving are capable of immense variation in the hands of a skilful worker, and many pretty borders, wreaths, and other designs may be adapted from it.

MAIDEN-HAIR FERN.

THIS design is simple of execution and yet very effective when nicely worked. The spray, as shown in our illustration, may be employed for the centre of a d'oyley, or several sprays may be grouped together in a pleasing manner to form a running border round a sideboard cloth, or be used for a toilet cover and other articles appertaining to a bedroom. Maiden hair fern combines well with almost any of the other sprays in this issue, and ladies who are skilful in designing for themselves will have no difficulty in selecting a suitable subject in which small sprays of maiden hair can with advantage be introduced. The whole of the fern leaves in our example are executed in flat satin stitch, the largest stitches being set longitudinally in the centre of the leaf, and graduating shorter on each side in a kind of triangular shape, as will be seen by reference to the engraving. The stem is worked throughout in snail trail stitch. Sometimes the leaves of maiden hair fern are worked in buttonhole stitch, the loops of the stitches making as it were a little ridge along the straight side of the leaf.

TOILET COVER.

DESIGN OF WHITE LILIES AND PASSION FLOWERS.

THIS toilet cover is a beautiful subject for Mountmellick

Wheat, Barley, and Grass.

Toilet Cover.

embroidery, and forms a really splendid and useful piece of work. The elaborate design of white lilies and passion flowers, as shown in the illustration, is embroidered upon a piece of white satin jean, measuring 44 inches wide by 17 inches deep. The work is carried 9 inches deep along the front of the cloth, and narrows at the sides; it is done with No. 8 knitting cotton. The toilet cover is handsomely finished off with scolloped buttonholing, and trimmed with the knitted fringe so extensively used for this style of work, than which nothing could be more appropriate, as it washes and wears as long as the work itself. Details of working white lilies and passion flowers appear each under their respective headings, accompanied by nearly full-size engravings of the subjects, and need not be repeated here. No difficulty whatever will be found in executing the design if the working instructions are strictly followed, both details and engravings being especially clear. A lovely arrangement for a bedroom might be made by working a quilt border, nightdress case, and comb bag to match.

Spray of Forget-me-nots.

Design of White Lilies and Passion Flowers.

SPRAY OF FORGET-ME-NOTS.

FORGET-ME-NOTS are an easy subject to work and invariably look pretty and attractive. In the example before us the flowers are executed in buttonhole stitch, five small petals forming a flower, and the stitches are taken moderately long in the centre of each petal and gradually shorter on each side where the petals are supposed to meet, and a tiny French knot is introduced in the centre to represent the eye of the flower. The leaves are small, and are of satin stitch worked over from side to side quite smoothly and evenly, or they may be slightly raised if desired like the one leaf that is shown on the lower branch of flowers. The stem being very fine and slender is most effectively imitated in back stitching. Forget-me-nots may also be worked to look well in raised satin stitch something after the manner of the blackberry flower delineated on page 13, of No. 45 of " Weldon's Practical Needlework Series," but of course smaller, and preserving the natural outline of the flower: in this case to give variety the leaves might be worked in flat satin stitch with a mid rib. Forget-me-nots mingle well with wild roses, jessamine, maidenhair fern, and other subjects. Briggs' transfer design, No. 226, of

in with trellis stitch elongated, as see illustration No. 41, in No. 45 of " Weldon's Practical Needlework Series," while from the margin of the leaf to this centre the work is executed in flat satin stitch, some of the stitches being longer than others to mark the indentations of the leaf. The stem is throughout embroidered in that peculiarly pretty stitch known as cable plait stitch, for explanation of working which, see page 5, No. 45 of " Weldon's Practical Needlework Series," where also will be found all the other stitches referred to in the present number.

GROUP OF WHITE LILIES.

THIS is a particularly handsome design, especially suitable for Mountmellick embroidery, and very effective. The lilies in our illustration are represented in nearly full working size, and are very thickly embroidered in French knots, working small knots to mark the outline of the petals and larger knots for filling in the centre, so that each petal may have a slightly rounded and re-curved appearance; the stamens are worked in crewel stitch, and each stamen has

Group of White Lilies.

Forget-me-nots and Narcissus would work out appropriately in Mountmellick for a wide handsome border, while the corner of the transfer pattern No. 581, design of Forget-me-nots, Rosebuds, and Jessamine, might be enlarged to serve for the corners of a dressing table cover, with an extension of the design along the front of the cloth.

SPRAY OF ROSE LEAVES.

ROSE LEAVES can be most effectively worked in Mountmellick embroidery. The small spray shown in our engraving affords a perfectly clear example of the manner of working, and would form a pretty centre for a d'oyley, or might be carried on in a series of sprays to form a handsome border, or be worked as a stripe or square for a counterpane or cot quilt. The leaves are broad, with serrated margin, as in the natural leaf, and the effect is heightened and conventionalised by a central space being left, which is afterwards filled

a single bullion stitch placed lengthways on the tip to simulate the anthers. The leaves are small in comparison with the flowers, and are designed so on purpose to give due prominence to the latter; they are of feather stitch—worked in the manner of the leaf No. 40, page 11, of No. 45 of " Weldon's Practical Needlework Series," but with a smooth edge. The stem is carried out in snail trail stitch. The design as shown in the engraving can be used for ornamenting the corners of a cloth, or may be duplicated and adapted for the centre of a tray cloth, or a series of groups could be nicely arranged to form a running border. The lilies in the toilet cover on pages 8 and 9 of this number are worked in the manner here represented, and with them passion flowers are mingled, forming together a natural and highly artistic arrangement. Wild roses, too, are an appropriate flower to combine in a design of white lilies, of course using leaves plentifully. and perhaps adding a blade of grass or an ear of wheat to occupy spaces and give an air of lightness to what might otherwise be a too heavy design.

Branch of Oak, with Oak Apple and Acorns.

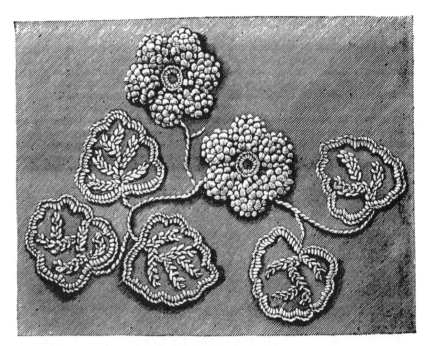

Double Marsh Marigolds and Leaves.

Toilet Mat. Design of Wild Roses and Corn.

BRANCH OF OAK, WITH OAK APPLE AND ACORNS.

THIS design is suitable to be continued for a border to go round a c t curtain, sideboard cloth, pillow sham, and other purposes. The thick braid-like appearance of the branch gives a particularly rich

Branch of Passion Flowers and Leaves.

and pleasing effect. On referring to the engraving, it will be seen that the branch is represented by an embroidery of cable plait stitch, and this stitch is illustrated in full size and complete details afforded of working, on page 5 of No. 45 of "Weldon's Practical Needlework Series," and need not be again explained here. Oak leaves have rugged edges, and these are beautifully imitated by an outline of French knots, with interior filling of crewel stitch, on either side of which here and there is worked a bullion stitch slanting to simulate the natural vein of the leaf. The oak apple is worked in thickly raised satin stitch, giving the appearance of a smooth spherical ball. The acorns are especially natural, the cup being composed of French knots worked thickly and closely together, while the nut, which is of satin stitch, is a little raised in the part which is close to the cup, and the stitches gradually narrow and get flatter as they approach the tip of the nut. Ladies who are skilful in designing will be able to plan out this subject in various ways, for instance, a larger and more spreading pattern, with a few blackberry leaves and blossoms added, will make a good design for a nightdress case and comb bag, so arranging that each is worked neither too close nor too far away from its neighbour, and that a free and natural bearing imparts breadth and boldness to the whole.

DOUBLE MARSH MARIGOLDS AND LEAVES.

NOTHING could be in better keeping with the style of Mountmellick embroidery than this pretty spray of double marsh marigolds and leaves. The broad flat leaves which are characteristic of the plant are most effectively represented by an outline of buttonhole stitch slightly curved to simulate the natural leaf, and filled with light

veinings worked in feather stitch. The flowers are particularly handsome, and as they are thickly raised they form a complete contrast to the flatness of the leaves; there are six petals in each flower, and these are carried out in French knots, small at the outer edge of the flower, and gradually larger as they approach the centre of the petal, while the eye of the flower is defined by a simple circle of buttonhole stitches. The stem is throughout worked in snail trail stitch, short stitches being taken, or small, short, outline stitches will be equally appropriate. Another arrangement of this subject appears in the brush and comb bag, page 5 of this issue, where its application to a useful purpose is at once perceivable. A nightdress case should be worked to match, and a toilet cloth will look well in the same pattern. Any one with a talent for embroidery will have no difficulty in arranging sprays of this pretty design to the size and shape of the article required to be made. Passion flowers and grasses mingle well with this design, and here and there a large fern leaf may be introduced, like the leaf on No. 42, on page 11 of No. 45 of "Weldon's Practical Needlework Series." Other pretty combinations may be elaborated according to fancy, working with intelligence, and keeping the whole as true to nature as possible.

TOILET MAT.

DESIGN OF WILD ROSES AND CORN.

THE graceful and pretty design represented in our engraving is worked for a toilet mat upon a piece of satin jean, oval in shape, and measuring from

Flower Leaf and Bud of Anemone Japonica.

10 to 12 inches long. The wild roses are executed in thickly raised satin stitch lengthway of the petals, of which there are five in each flower, with a group of three or four small French knots in the centre. The buds are partly of raised and partly of flat satin stitch, the narrow pointed segments being

raised work. The leaves are variously rendered, and here great taste is displayed, one spray is outlined with French knots and embellished with bullion stitch veining, and another spray similarly outlined is filled in with trellis stitch, while the spray to the right is embroidered in flat satin stitch worked simply across from side to side of each leaf, and the spray to the left is entirely in close feather stitch. The corn is portrayed in bullion stitch single and double, with a straight spike stitch on the tip of each ear to simulate the "beard." The blade of grass is defined by overcast stitch. The stems are worked partly in outline stitch and partly in snail trail stitch. The mat is bordered with the scolloped buttonhole stitch so peculiarly appropriate to Mountmellick embroidery, and is edged with the popular knitted fringe.

BRANCH OF PASSION FLOWERS AND LEAVES.

THIS subject lends itself most favourably for reproduction in

with a mid rib of good-sized French knots; the upper leaf has a line of small French knots worked closely together round the margin and is filled in with trellis stitch expanded to shape; other ways of working leaves will present themselves as one gets proficient in the work; as a rule, the more variety that can be produced in a large piece of work the better will be the effect. Passion flower petals are generally embroidered over and over from side to side in flat or only slightly raised satin stitch, the arc, or corona, is represented by a circle or a half-circle (as the flower appears more or less full) of bullion stitches, for method of arranging which see the engraving, while a description of the manner of working the stitches will be found on page 6, of No. 45 of "Weldon's Practical Needlework Series." The centre of the flower is of satin stitch highly raised and from this centre proceeds five small stamens composed of one or two outline stitches each stamen surmounted by a tiny French knot to represent the anther.

Passion flowers combine well with white lilies and maidenhair fern. Those who like to work from a transfer pattern will find Briggs'

Spray of Fuchsia.

Mountmellick embroidery, and with its lovely flowers, deeply-cut leaves, and graceful tendrils set upon a climbing stem, invariably looks as pretty and natural as well can be desired. Our engraving depicts a branch of passion flowers and leaves in almost full working size and as almost every stitch is visible the manner of working is clearly apparent. Passion flowers worked thus are introduced in the Nightdress Case, pages 8-9 in No. 45 of "Weldon's Practical Needlework Series," and also in the toilet cover, page 8 and 9 of the present issue; and the above example may be enlarged and extended to form a border for a bed quilt, curtains, and other purposes. The method of enlarging a design and tracing a pattern on material is explained at the commencement of the present number. The stem may be successfully carried out in crewel stitch, cording stitch, and chain stitch, varied to taste, and using snail trail stitch for the tendrils. The lower leaf in the example before us is buttonhole-stitched round the outline, while the centre of each section is ornamented

transfer pattern No. 362 a very good design for a fairly wide border of passion flowers.

FLOWER, LEAF, AND BUD OF ANEMONE JAPONICA.

THE lovely flowers of the anemone japonica can be skilfully portrayed as shown in our illustration. These flowers have five petals, and by referring to the engraving it will be seen that these petals are worked in flat satin stitch in two divisions, so that the stitches from each side meet down the middle and form an indented line or vein; the centre of the flower is composed of a cluster of seven French knots, round which is a circlet or "ray" of bullion stitches, to represent the "ray" of the natural flower. The effect of the bullion stitches, in combination with French knots and flat satin stitch, is particularly pleasing. The bud is worked entirely in French knots, larger knots being made in the centre than at the margin, the stem upon which the bud depends is chain stitch. The stem of the flower is worked in cable stitch (see No. 6, page 5, in No. 45 of " Weldon's Practical Needlework Series "), and the stem of the leaf is double cable stitch, which is detailed on the page just referred to. The leaf, which is large, is outlined with a row of French knots, and the veining is carried out in cable plait stitch, a particularly pleasing stitch, instruction for working which will also be found in our previous issue. A lovely design for a sideboard cloth or five-o'clock tea-cloth can be arranged from this pretty flower, and fern and ivy may appropriately be mingled with it.

SPRAY OF FUCHSIA.

A SPRAY of fuchsia with its graceful pendulous flowers is an appropriate subject for Mountmellick embroidery, and looks well mingled with wild roses, passion flowers, double marsh marigolds, and other subjects, and these can be combined in a design suitable for a toilet table cover, brush and comb bag, pillow sham, &c., or sprays of fuchsia can be arranged to form by themselves a wide and handsome border

twined with a branch of oak leaves and acorns. The methods of working ivy leaves are very various, in fact they may be carried out entirely according to taste, even working the leaves upon the same spray in different manners, as shown in our engraving. The leaf at the top of the spray to the right is outlined with French knots, and the veining is of outline stitch and bullion stitches ; the leaf to the left is done in flat satin stitch, worked in two divisions, and the stitches meeting in the centre, form a kind of natural indentation representing the vein ; two of the small leaves are worked in this same manner, while the large pointed leaf on the right-hand side of the example and the small leaf in the centre are worked in feather stitch, in the same way as the leaf shown by illustration 40, page 11, in No. 45 of " Weldon's Practical Needlework Series," but with an even edge. The small leaf to the left is outlined with French knots and filled in with a few long stitches, and the leaf at the bottom of the stem is worked entirely in French knots, those in the veining being rather larger than the knots round the margin ; the tiny stems which lead to each separate leaf are depicted by snail trail stitch, while the main portion of the stem is crewel stitch, worked double in the thickest part of the stem, and with a few spike stitches branching out here and there to represent the little fibrous rootlets seen in natural ivy.

Ivy Leaves.

that will look well for a counterpane and bedhangings, and other purposes. Our engraving shows clearly a natural branch of the flower, and the manner in which the work is executed. The three fuchsias have each their sepals and corolla embroidered in satin stitch, slightly raised, and worked over from side to side of each section ; the stamens of the two outside flowers are worked in snail trail stitch, while in the centre flower these are simulated in outline or crewel stitch, and each stamen has one small French knot at the end to represent the anther. The buds also are of satin stitch slightly raised. The leaves, which are long and rather narrow, with a slightly serrated edge, are worked in flake stitch. For details and example of working, see illustration 37, page 11, of No. 45 of " Weldon's Practical Needlework Series."

IVY LEAVES.

THE ivy leaf lends itself favourably to reproduction in Mountmellick embroidery, and may form an entire design of itself, or a few leaves may be introduced in an arrangement of passion flowers and lilies or of wild roses and forget-me-nots, or may be prettily

WELDON'S PRACTICAL
MOUNTMELLICK EMBROIDERY

(THIRD SERIES.)

New and Original Designs for Toilet Covers, Pincushions, Quilts, Brush and Comb Bags; also Grouped Sprays for Decorative Purposes.

SEVENTEEN ILLUSTRATIONS.

MOUNTMELLICK EMBROIDERY.

WE now place before our readers our third issue on Mountmellick Embroidery, feeling sure that the ladies who have taken so much interest in working from the two previous numbers will be pleased with a further selection of new designs for this charming variety of useful fancy work. Unlike most other kinds of fancy work, it is strong and durable, washes perfectly, and really looks well to the last; it also is a work one never gets tired of seeing, therefore it is particularly suitable for sideboard cloths, five-o'clock tea-slips, and bedroom accessories. The present issue contains valuable designs for working a nightdress sachet, brush and comb bag, duchesse table cloth, and a corner for a quilt, also designs for several lovely borders and sprays, &c. Other handsome subjects are illustrated and fully explained in No. 47 of "Weldon's Practical Needlework Series," while No. 45 is devoted to preliminary instructions regarding the different stitches made use of in this fascinating work, all of which are fully illustrated and described, together with a few simple examples of the uses to which they can be turned, and also a lovely nightdress case in a design of passion flowers and asters. The three numbers together form the most complete arrangement of Mountmellick Embroidery that has hitherto been published.

Coat of Arms.

COAT OF ARMS.

A COAT of Arms forms an appropriate subject to place in the centre of a quilt, at the corner of a pillow sham, upon a nightdress sachet, or on any piece of work where such a design will look well.

It is, of course, not intended that the accompanying illustration should be copied in detail, it is given rather as an example of the purposes to which Mountmellick Embroidery can be applied, and to afford an idea to be adapted to a family coat of arms, or may be varied to represent a shield. It may either be worked straight upon the article it is purposed to adorn, or it may be executed upon a separate piece of satin jean, and placed in position when complete. The outline in either case should be worked in button-hole stitching over one or two strands of coarse cotton to raise the stitching well above the level of the foundation; the quarterings may be defined with crewel stitch, chain stitch, or cable stitch, or any other stitches the worker can successfully master.

NIGHTDRESS SACHET.
DESIGN OF OAK LEAVES AND ACORNS, GRASSES, THISTLES, MARGUERITES, AND BUTTERFLIES.

THE accompanying design represents a nightdress sachet executed in Mountmellick Embroidery in a combination of subjects, conventionally treated, and producing altogether a particularly effective and pleasing piece of work. The foundation is of white satin jean material of the best quality, of which rather more than three-quarters of a yard will be required, and must be cut into three pieces, allowing a piece 13 inches long by 18 inches wide for the back of the sachet, a piece 10 inches long by 18 inches wide for the front, and a piece 4½ inches long by 18 inches wide for the flap. Trace the design upon the front of the sachet, and on the flap, as shown in the illustration; the procedure of enlarging and tracing a design is explicitly detailed on page 4, No. 47, of "Weldon's Practical Needlework Series," which is entirely devoted to handsome designs for Mountmellick Embroidery, as also is No. 45, and the two numbers are obtainable through any bookseller or fancy repository, price 2d. each, or from this office for 2½d. each, post free. The back of the sachet is quite plain. Use

Bring up the needle and cotton close by the cable plait, insert the needle to take up a few threads of the material about half-an-inch distant and in a nearly straight direction, and draw through, then pass the needle and cotton twice or three times round the long stitch just formed, and finally return the needle to the back of the work a mere thread or two from where the stitch started; work seven or eight more stitches in the same manner, making some longer and some shorter, as shown in the engraving. The leaf has a serrated edge and is worked in flake stitch. Proceed next with the spray of marguerites in the right-hand corner of the flap. The stem is formed of couching stitch worked over one strand of cotton, and consequently is more slender than the stem in the spray of

Nightdress Sachet. Design of Oak Leaves and Acorns, Grasses, Thistles, Marguerites, and Butterflies.

Strutt's knitting cotton No. 6 and No. 8, for working the flowers and leaves, and No. 12 for the butterflies.

Commence with the flap, on which work first the spray of thistles in the left-hand corner. This consists of a stem, three flowers, and one leaf; the stem is executed in couching stitch, with three strands of coarse cotton laid down to work upon, and when this is done, a line of small spike stitches is added at regular intervals along each side of the couching; the thistles are prettily outlined with cable plait stitch, from which, at the top, springs a tuft of long twisted stitches, and the remaining portion of the outline is embellished with spike stitch similar to the spike stitches on the stem, while the interior is occupied with French knots dotted not too closely together. The long twisted stitches are worked thus—

thistles; the leaves are long and thin, and are worked simply in flake stitch from the base to the tip; the flowers are prettily devised with a centre or eye composed of a cluster of small French knots, surrounded by a circle of numerous petals, which are simulated by working long bullion stitches in pairs, and afterwards connecting the pairs together by inserting a tiny French knot close to their tips. The butterfly is first of all traced entire on a piece of fine cambric muslin, then the outline of four wings is worked in small button-hole stitch overcasting, using No. 12 cotton. Nothing as yet is done upon a very narrow rib of material that must be left vacant between the wings for the future working of the body, but you proceed to fill up the wings, decorating each with a tiny circlet of button-hole stitches to simulate the coloured blotches usually seen on butterflies' wings, and the remainder of the space is filled with ornamental stitches, as flat satin stitch, feather stitch, outline stitch, and French knots, all of which are clearly visible in the illustration; when complete lay the butterfly in position upon the centre of the flap of the nightdress sachet, and work the body in highly raised satin stitch in such a way that the wings are attached to the satin jean by the process of working the raised satin stitch over the narrow line of cambric that has hitherto been left void between the wings. The wings now are in two sections, and are moveable from the satin jean; work a small cluster of French knots to represent the head of the butterfly and add two long spike stitches to simulate the antennæ; this completes the Mountmellick Embroidery for the flap. A bold spray of oak leaves and acorns occupies the left-hand side of the front of the nightdress sachet; here the principal stem is worked in thick couching, while the smaller stems are represented variously in thin couching, small close overcasting, and snail-trail stitch; there are six leaves, of which only four are visible in the engraving, the other two being concealed under the fringe; the large leaf in the corner is outlined with button-hole stitch worked over a foundation thread, and the veining is composed of French knots; the leaf to the right is defined with a double margin of French knots, and copiously filled with crewel-stitch veining. The serrated leaf, still further to the right, is a pretty leaf, outlined with cable plait stitch, with small veinings worked in crewel stitch, snail - trail stitch, and feather stitch, tastefully blended; the small leaf to the left is represented with an outline of cable stitch and veining of crewel stitch, while of the two other small leaves hidden beneath the fringe, one is worked with a couched outline and the other defined with an outline of cable - plait stitch, and both are ornamented with a veining of feather stitch. The acorns are beautifully executed, all in highly raised work, and each one

snail-trail stitch, and bullion stitch, as represented in the engraving. The butterfly in the right-hand corner is worked in the same manner as the butterfly on the flap, the wings only being just a little differently filled in with honeycomb stitch, feather stitch, crewel stitch, and French knots. The scallops of the nightdress case are worked round with indented button-hole stitching, and a straight line of the same is used to finish off the top of the front (under the flap), and the top of the sachet; this can be done at pleasure, either before or after the Mount-mellick Embroidery is worked. Cut away the surplus material from the outside

Corner for a Quilt. Design of Vine Leaves and Grapes.

varying in detail; for instance, some of the nuts are composed of highly raised satin stitch and some of raised bullion stitches worked across from side to side. The cups are prettily fashioned in good contrasting style; an acorn with a nut worked in satin stitch has a cup of raised bullion stitches worked longitudinally; other cups are composed of large French knots massed thickly and closely together, and two or three acorns with nuts of raised satin stitches worked down to meet the stem, have their cups embroidered in a kind of honeycombed network, apart from, yet lying closely around the nut. The grasses are tastefully worked in couching stitch, crewel stitch,

of the scallops, and make up the sachet in the usual manner, joining the pieces neatly together. A border of knitted fringe is used for trimming, which is worked as follows: Wind a supply of No. 12 knitting cotton upon four separate balls, and use from all four balls together, working with a pair of No. 11 steel knitting needles. Cast on 12 stitches. **1st row**—Make 1 (by passing all four strands of cotton round the needle), knit 2 together, knit 1, and repeat this three times. Every row is the same. When you have knitted a sufficient length to go nicely round the article you intend trimming, cast off 7 stitches, break off the cotton, and draw the end through the last stitch on the right-hand needle. Slip the 5 remaining stitches off the left-hand needle, and unravel them all the way along, and a pretty crinkled fringe will be produced. Sew the fringe by the loop stitches that are at the top of the heading to the edge of the indented button-hole stitching that borders the nightdress case.

This fringe is fully illustrated and detailed in No. 45 of "Weldon's Practical Needlework Series," which contains all the preliminary instructions for this most attractive and durable of Needleworks.

An elegantly designed Nightdress Case of Passion Flowers and Asters appears in No. 45 of "Weldon's Practical Needlework Series."

CORNER FOR A QUILT.
DESIGN IN VINE LEAVES AND GRAPES.

THIS elegant design of vine leaves and grapes is intended for working on the four corners of a quilt, and should extend from 36 inches to 40 inches along each side from the corner. As satin jean is not manufactured wider than 32 inches or 36 inches from selvedge to selvedge, three widths must be joined together to make a quilt.

The method of enlarging and tracing a design is fully explained on page 4, No. 47, of "Weldon's Practical Needlework Series," and need not again be repeated. The stem throughout the design now under consideration is worked in cable stitch (for description of which see illustration 6, page 5, No. 45, of "Weldon's Practical Needlework Series"); two lines of cable stitch are arranged closely parallel to simulate the thickest portion of the stem, or rather to form that part of the stem that represents the branch of the vine, and a single line denotes the stems leading to the leaves and the grapes. The tendrils are all executed in crewel stitch, or may be variously worked in cording stitch and in snail-trail stitch. The leaves throughout are alike embroidered with an outline of French knots and a copious filling of feather stitch, and the grapes are prettily outlined with a margin of cable-plait stitch (see illustration 8, page 5, No. 45, "Weldon's Practical Needlework Series") and a centre filling composed of two bullion stitches placed thus ( ).

The centre of the quilt may be ornamented with the owner's crest, or coat-of-arms, or with a flight of swallows, or with cog-wheel rings (see page 12, No. 45, of "Weldon's Practical Needlework Series") dotted about at intervals about six inches apart from each other. The sides and the top and bottom of the quilt are worked in deep button-hole stitching in large scallops, the head of the button-hole stitching is decorated with a scalloped line of bullion stitches, as is clearly apparent by reference to the engraving; and the quilt is finished with a border of the knitted fringe, fully described at end of description of Nightdress Sachet, on page 5 of this issue, and which forms such an appropriate trimming for all articles of Mountmellick Embroidery.

SPRAY OF IVY, COBWEB AND SPIDERS.

THIS is a lovely design, and may be utilised for various purposes. If worked exactly as represented in the illustration, it is suitable for a d'oyley, cheese cloth, or small tray cloth or the spray of ivy may be enlarged and continued, adding here and there more leaves, and another spider, or a small cobweb, till the design is brought to a size sufficiently large for a nightdress sachet or a pillow sham; it also may be still more enlarged, and a spray or two of passion flowers

and grasses introduced, to form a splendid design for a duchesse table-cloth or a five o'clock tea-table slip.

The stem, as shown in our engraving, is worked in close overcast stitches well raised over a couching of three or four strands of cotton. All the tendrils are simulated by snail-trail stitch, which so easily lends itself to graceful curves. The centre leaf is first of all highly raised with padding darned forwards and backwards within the allotted space, and then worked smoothly and thickly in long satin stitches, the stitches reaching from the margin on each side to the centre of the leaf, where they meet and form an indented line or mid-rib. There are two leaves at the top of the spray, one of which is worked in darning stitch, and the other is outlined with cable-plait stitch, and filled with an ample veining of crewel stitch. The large leaf at the bottom of the spray is formed of heavy raised darning stitch, and the other leaf is prettily outlined with French knots and filled in with feather stitch. Next proceed with the spider at the top of the spray, and work the body smoothly and evenly in raised satin stitch; the head is simulated by three French knots grouped closely together, the horns by tiny spike stitches, and the legs are simply loose threads of cotton in which, previously to inserting the needle, two knots have been tied to represent the joints in the legs. The other spider is worked in the same way, but is not quite so large. The spider's web is commenced by working eight long stitches in the form of a star, at equal distances one from the other, as shown in the engraving. The centre is then darned round and round, over one thread and under one thread, and in each successive round going over the thread you before went under, till a circle about the size of a sixpence is closely worked, when fasten off neatly; the same stitch is employed to work four rounds with a space left between each round, which completes the web.

Spray of Ivy. Cobweb and Spiders.

GROUP OF BULRUSHES AND A MOTH.

A GRACEFUL and pretty design of bulrushes is a favourite subject for Mountmellick Embroidery, and invariably looks natural and pleasing. The subject of the annexed engraving may be employed for traycloths and d'oyleys, and ladies who are skilful in designing will be able to carry the same on to a larger and more spreading pattern, and by the addition of sprays of double marsh marigolds (see page 11, No. 47, of "Weldon's Practical Needlework Series"), or water-lilies and rushes, as worked upon the brush and comb-bag, page 11 of the present issue, a lovely design can be arranged, suitable for a toilet cover or sideboard slip. The stems of the bulrushes are worked in snail-trail stitch, but may equally well be produced in crewel stitch or cording stitch, according to fancy. The leaves are thin and long, and are worked in overcast stitching, either flat or raised, as preferred. The rushes are beautifully executed in fluffy rug stitch, which is worked in a parallel direction from left to right, over a netting mesh about three-quarters of an inch wide, or a slip of stout cardboard cut to the same width will serve the purpose; bring up the needle and cotton on the outline of the bulrush on the right side of the material, hold the mesh upon the material, keeping it in place by pressure of the left-hand thumb, pass the cotton over the mesh, then under, and take two small stitches into the material to secure the loop. Every stitch is worked in the same way, and when the length of the bulrush is completed the mesh is drawn out, the cotton is fastened off, and another row is worked in the same manner quite close to the row that has just been done; when sufficient rug stitch is accomplished to cover the surface of the bulrush, the cotton is cut, and combed out and clipped to the shape, desired. Bulrushes are also very properly worked in French knots, and sometimes in bullion stitch. The moth is embroidered in finer cotton than is used for the other portion of the design; the outline is worked in chain stitch, then the wings and the head are formed with a few very tiny French knots and feather stitches, and two spike stitches project from the head to simulate horns.

CHRYSANTHEMUMS.

Arranged for a Border.

This is a very handsome design, and though executed for the most part in a novel and pretty arrangement of stitches is not beyond the capability of a fairly experienced worker. Chrysanthemums may otherways be arranged to form a solid all-over pattern for working on nightdress sachets, and for other purposes; or a few ears of wheat, barley, and grasses may be introduced, and the whole arranged in a tasteful design to suit the size and shape of the article it is intended to adorn.

The chrysanthemum stem, as shown in our engraving, is worked entirely in fine close overcast stitching. The first leaf at the bottom of the stem at the right-hand side is prettily executed in two sections; the upper section is of close evenly-worked satin stitch raised on a slightly padded foundation the needle being so placed as to slant the stitches from the mid-rib to the margin of the leaf; the under-section is composed of a series of bullion stitches worked in the form of spikes extending from the mid-rib to the other margin of the leaf. The upper division of the next leaf is embroidered in elongated trellis stitch (for instruction in working see page 11, No. 45, "Weldon's Practical Needlework Series"), it has a mid-rib of overcast stitch, and the lower division is outlined with small button-hole stitches, between which and the mid-rib runs a row of French knots of graduated sizes, the smaller knots being towards the tip of the leaf. Work the petals of the full-blown flower in slightly raised satin stitch, and fill the centre with a cluster of French knots. The leaf next above is tastefully executed with a row of spiked stitches

Group of Bulrushes and a Moth.

carried along its upper section, each spike stitch being dotted on the tip with a French knot, while the lower portion of the leaf is entirely composed of French knots, small, and arranged quite closely together. The three chrysanthemum buds are all worked similarly with petals of flat satin or overcast stitches and base of French knots. The leaf at the top of the stem is outlined with overcast stitch, a mid-rib of the same passes up the centre of the leaf, which then is completed with a filling of diamond stitch worked quite evenly and held in place by one small bind stitch confining the cross threads of each diamond. The small leaf on the left-hand side is neatly delineated with overcast stitching, and in the centre, taking the place of a mid-rib, is a line of four wafer-like spots worked in slightly raised satin stitch. The next leaf is most tastefully elaborated in two sections, the one section being worked in thick raised satin stitch graduated in length to the formation of the leaf, and the other section occupied with rows of small loops of button-hole stitches worked upon a thread of cotton as if making the loops used upon dresses. The large wide leaf next demands attention, and is simply worked with an outline of cable-plait stitch, and an ample veining of crewel stitch. The very small leaf worked close

---

DUCHESSE TABLE CLOTH.

Design of Poppies and Honeysuckle Sprays.

The toilet cloth shown in our engraving is specially adapted for a duchesse table, and the original measures 54 inches long and 16 inches deep, and is shaped a little at the back to accord with the table it is destined to cover. Most cloths for duchesse tables would be shaped in the same way, unless a long straight slip fringed all round is preferred. The material selected for the cloth is white satin jean, of the best quality, and the work is executed with No. 8 knitting cotton, in a simple yet pretty design of poppies and honeysuckle. The poppies are grouped together in the centre of the cloth, and again at each corner, and the intermediate space, and also a small space on each side, is occupied with honeysuckle. The centre spray consists of two full blown poppies, three buds, and three seed pods, and leaves of different sizes. Work the stems according to taste in cable-plait stitch, cable stitch, and snail-trail stitch. The large flower to the right has five petals all outlined with snail-trail stitch and filled with good-sized French knots, the centre of the flower is composed of a circle of French knots grouped closely together, and round this is an almost circular ray of bullion stitches with just a few flat satin stitches breaking the circle at the base of the flower. The petals of the other large flower are outlined with crewel stitch and filled with French knots, while the centre is formed by a round spot of thickly raised satin stitch, from which extends an "arc" of spike stitches that would be circular were it not broken into by a few flat satin stitches worked near the junction of the stem. The seed pods are effectively executed in French knots worked thickly and closely together, and a tuft of long indented satin stitches protrudes as it were from the mouth of the pod in the manner shown in the engraving. Some of the buds are larger than others, but all are worked in the same way in raised satin stitches in two unequal-sized divisions or sections, the larger section being the most raised, the buds are supposed to be just bursting forth, and a few stitches of flat satin stitch are inserted in such a manner as to represent the opening. The leaves are variously worked—the large leaf to the right is outlined with small French knots and filled with a copious veining of crewel stitch and bullion stitches; the other leaf is also defined by a margin of French knots, and is completed with a veining of crewel stitch and double bullion stitches; while the leaf to the left-hand side is worked in the same manner as the leaf to the right. The other leaves are embroidered in simple flat satin stitch, taking the stitches in two divisions, and of different lengths, to simulate a serrated edge; the working of the stitches forms of itself a kind of mid-rib down the centre of the leaf. All the tendrils are worked in snail-trail stitch. The poppy sprays at each corner are worked in style to correspond with the centre spray. The

upon the stem of the bud is defined with small overcast stitches, the same stitches being used for a mid-rib up the centre of the leaf. The leaf at the bottom of the stem, opposite the first leaf, is embroidered in two divisions, the lower division is outlined and partially filled with indented satin stitch, and the upper division after being outlined with crewel stitch, is entirely filled with rows of tiny close back stitching.

honeysuckle sprays are very easy to work, and consist of leaves only, as this portion of the design is secondary to the flowers and leaves of the poppy sprays, and therefore must not be made too conspicuous; the stem is of cording stitch, and the leaves raised satin stitch, for the mode of working which see page 11, No. 45, of "Weldon's Practical Needlework Series," where a spray of honeysuckle is depicted in nearly full working size

The table-cloth is edged round three sides with an edging of saw-tooth, button-holing, and on the fourth side (which is the back of the cloth) with plain button-holing. Then the cloth is completed by the addition of a handsome knitted fringe, described at foot of design of Nightdress Sachet, on page 5. A handsomely designed Toilet Cover of White Lilies and Passion Flowers appears in No. 47 of "Weldon's Practical Needlework Series."

Chrysanthemums Arranged for a Border.

ORANGES.
CONVENTIONAL DESIGN FOR A BORDER.

THE oranges represented in our engraving are a very effective subject for a border, which may be from eight inches to fourteen or sixteen inches wide. The stem winds alternately from right to left, and is worked throughout in close firm overcast stitch, and great care should be taken that the stitches lie smoothly side by side, closely together, yet not in the least overlapping each other. The leaves afford a good example of the variety obtainable in Mount-mellick Embroidery, almost every known stitch being called into requisition. We will describe each leaf separately in rotation, beginning at the bottom of the stem. A very pretty leaf is that on the

right-hand side, with the outline worked in fine overcast stitch round which runs an edge of very tiny French knots, and up the centre of the leaf occupying the place of a mid-rib, is a line of six wafer-like spots, worked in raised satin stitch. The next leaf is quite different in style, being embroidered in two sections or divisions, the lower section is composed entirely of raised satin stitches, slanting from the outside to the centre of the leaf, while the upper section is simply outlined with crewel stitch along the margin, and filled with small French knots worked at intervals in a line from the base to the tip of the leaf. The third leaf on the right-hand side is defined with an outline of cable-plait stitch, and filled in with a mid-rib and veining of crewel stitch. The next leaf is formed simply of two rows of flake stitch extending from the outside to the centre of the leaf where a mid-rib of crewel stitch is afterwards put in. The next is an elaborate leaf, one half being of raised satin stitch and the other half being outlined with small fine overcasting and worked with diamond filling. The top leaf is defined with button-hole stitching, it has a mid-rib of cable-plait stitch, and on each side between this and the button-hole stitching is an ornamental line of French knots running from the base to the top of the leaf. The small leaf on the left-hand side is composed entirely of bullion stitches, worked very evenly in a slanting direction from the margin to the centre of the

Duchesse Dressing-Table Cover

leaf, where the stitches meet and form a natural vein. The next is a pretty leaf. One side of it is formed of satin stitches of various lengths, the indentations being arranged to come on the inside instead of as usual on the margin of the leaf; the mid-rib is of closely worked overcast stitch, and the other side of the leaf is worked in trellis stitch expanded to the required shape. The next leaf is handsomely worked, and, from its novel effect, will repay careful attention. It is divided into two sections; one section is composed of small French knots, all exactly the same size, worked closely together, while the other section is embroidered in rows of small loops of button-hole stitch, thus ⌣, in the same way that the loops are made that are sometimes placed for the fastenings of dresses. The leaf next below is worked on one side with the indented satin stitch described in a previous leaf, and it has a mid-rib of close firm overcasting, from which a line of bullion stitches extend as far as the opposite outline of the leaf. The oranges are not difficult of execution, but care must be taken in tracing to get them a correct shape. The illustration shows four different styles of working oranges, and other combinations of stitches may be invented as the work proceeds, or the same may be repeated over and over again for the length of the border. The rim of the first orange is defined by a circle of cable-plait stitch, inside which is worked four circles of crewel stitch each at a little distance one from the other; the orange is then completed by the addition of a few ornamental stitches depending from the stem. The second orange has its outer rib delineated with button-hole stitch, then a circle of French knots about the size of a threepenny piece is worked in the middle of the orange, and from this the space as far as the outer rim is filled with a series of long stitches radiating from the circle of French knots towards the button-hole stitching, and these long threads are ornamented with lace stitches, grouping them together in clusters of four threads, as will be seen by reference to the engraving. The third orange is prettily surrounded with cable-plait stitch, and filled in with a double circle of round wafer-like spots, worked in slightly raised satin stitch. The fourth orange is outlined with crewel stitch, beyond which is an edging of small French knots, and the centre is tastefully occupied by a circle of crewel stitch, with long spike stitches radiating therefrom, each spike stitch being finished off with a French knot at the tip.

SUNFLOWERS.

OUR engraving shows a design of sunflowers adapted for a border, and worked in a very effective style, in a combination of the many pretty stitches applicable to this description of art needlework; both flowers and leaves are large and bold, and therefore the subject is

sign of Poppies and Honeysuckle Sprays.

well suited to Mountmellick Embroidery, and ladies who are clever in sketching will be able to re-arrange the same in various forms for working upon toilet covers, nightdress cases, and brush and comb bags, or for pillow shams and quilts.

The stalk of the sunflower, which for the most part is thick and solid, is worked throughout in cable-plait stitch, and the stems belonging to each leaf and flower, being thinner, are successfully represented by snail-trail stitch and cable stitch—these three stitches will be found illustrated in full working size on page 5, No. 45, of "Weldon's Practical Needlework Series." The leaf at the bottom of the stalk on the right-hand side is outlined with button-hole stitch, the stitches being taken a little apart from each other, and the veining which occupies nearly all the centre of the leaf is worked in feather stitch. The leaf at the top is depicted with a line of small French knots worked closely together round the margin, and is filled entirely with the pretty stitch known as honeycomb stitch; for details see pages 9 and 10, No. 45, of "Weldon's Practical Needlework Series," which is the first issue on Mountmellick Embroidery, and contains all the elementary stitches. The large leaf to the left is simply worked with an outline of French knots, and a mid-rib of crewel stitch, and veining of long bullion stitches. The full-blown flower on the right-hand side of the stalk has petals of bullion stitches worked evenly across from side to side, the stitches vary in length, and of course get quite short as they approach the tip of

each petal; the centre of the flower, that is, the part that is usually full of seeds, is composed of good-sized French knots worked with thicker cotton than that employed for the petals, or a double cotton is sometimes used, but in this event great care must be taken to get the two threads to draw together with just the same degree of tightness. The top flower is composed of petals worked in satin stitch, highly raised, the satin stitches being embroidered from side

Oranges. Conventional Design for a Border.

to side over a padded foundation, and graduated in size to the contour of the tracing, a circlet of bullion stitches is then worked closely and firmly for filling in the middle of the flower.

Briggs' Transfer design, No. 329, of sunflowers for a border, will work out very effectively in Mountmellick Embroidery in the stitches that are here described, or in any other combination of stitches that may be preferred.

THREE-SIDED COMB AND BRUSH BAG.

Design of Water Lily and Bulrushes.

Our illustration represents a comb and brush bag of novel shape, which being made with three sides is more roomy and capacious than bags made with two sides only, besides being much prettier. It is composed of three pieces of the best white satin jean, each piece measuring 14 inches long and 7 inches wide. Cut a piece of paper to the shape shown in the engraving, and outline the same upon each piece of material, and work down each side and the bottom of the bag with indented button-holing, after which the outer margin of material is cut away. The work is executed with Strutt's No. 10 knitting cotton. Trace on each piece of material the design of water lily and bulrushes as in the engraving, making some little alteration in the arrangement, so that all three sides may present a pleasing variation of the idea. The leaf of the water lily is outlined partly in button-hole stitch and partly in French knots, and veined with cording stitch and feather stitch. The flower stands as it were *upon* the leaf, and, by clever manipulation of the stitches, appears as if raised therefrom. The petals are first of all thickly padded with darning and then worked in satin stitch over and over from side to side, and the centre is filled with a circlet of bullion stitches placed quite thickly and closely together. A few lines of crewel stitches give the appearance of water. There are two bulrushes and two blades of grass upon the side of the bag selected for representation. The bulrush to the right is worked across from side to side in close even rows of bullion stitches, and tapered off to a point at the top with a few overcast stitches and one spike stitch, and the stem is depicted by a line of crewel stitch. The other bulrush is embroidered entirely in French knots, the head tapered with overcast stitches and a spike stitch, and the stem worked in snail-trail stitch. Both blades of grass are defined by overcast stitching.

On the other sides of the bag the work may be carried out in a slightly different style; for instance, the bulrushes may both be worked in French knots or both in bullion stitch, and the outlining of the water-lily leaf may be cable-plait stitch, or cable plait and overcasting combined, which pretty stitch is shown on page 6, No. 45, of "Weldon's Practical Needlework Series," where also will be found instructions for working all the different stitches to which allusion is made in this present issue.

The three sides of the bag are sewn together by the edge of the button-hole stitches at the same time as the fringe (which should be previously knitted) is put on. The top of the bag is finished off with a narrow hem. A tape is laid in position below the hem, on the inside of the bag, to contain drawing strings, and is held in place by two rows of French knots, as will be seen by the engraving.

A nightdress sachet, with a design of water lilies and bulrushes, should be made to use with the bag.

A differently shaped Brush and Comb Bag in a design of Marsh Marigolds appears in No. 47 of "Weldon's Practical Needlework Series."

Sunflowers.

A SWALLOW.

This bird lends itself most favourably for reproduction in Mountmellick Embroidery, and is a very useful subject for working upon a table cover, pillow sham, or cot quilt, in combination with a simple spray of flowers and leaves, or a group of bulrushes and grasses. A flight of five or six swallows makes a splendid centre for a bed spread; they should vary in size, the largest bird being placed as leader of the flight, and the others following in gradation. Our illustration is taken from a swallow beautifully executed in highly raised work, and measuring from five to six inches from head to tail.

The outline of the swallow should be traced in the usual manner. Then the body is darned over and over with thick cotton till it stands as highly raised as is desired, most particularly so in the top wing, the upper part of the body, and the top of the head over the eye, for which a space or hollow should be left to receive one French knot, which can be put in when the body of the bird is completed. The head is worked in satin stitch; the beak is composed of a few small flat satin stitches. The upper portions of the wings are elaborated of long twisted stitches, or flake stitches, alternated with bullion stitches of medium length, and prettily mingled together; and one or two very long bullion stitches (unpadded) stretch down quite to the extreme end of the wings. It is rather difficult at first to get into the way of working these very long stitches as round and as roll-like as they should be, but practice will lead to perfection. The tail is worked in loose large chain stitches. The swallow looks most effective if not too fine cotton be employed in the working, No. 6 is not any too coarse for large birds such as would be used on a bed spread or pillow sham, while No. 8 will do nicely for all other purposes.

Several good designs of swallow and other birds can be obtained in Briggs' series of patent transfer papers in full size for working. These are most convenient for ladies not wishing to design for themselves, as they are readily transferred by means of a warm iron.

SPRAY OF POMEGRANATE.

A design of pomegranates forms a good subject for Mountmellick Embroidery, and is very suitable for the borders and corners of quilts, for curtains, five-o'clock teacloths, and any purpose for which a bold important looking design is required. The spray shown in our illustration may be employed as a powdering, dotted here and there over the entire surface of the material, and also will serve as a guide for designing and working a running border, while three sprays prettily grouped together will form a corner.

The stem of the pomegranate, which is rather thick, is effectively represented by a series of close even overcast stitches from which, at intervals, spike stitches are worked jutting out to simulate the hairy fibres of the natural stem. The leaf to the left at the bottom of the stem is outlined with small button-hole stitches and the veining is worked in crewel stitch. Above this leaf will be seen two small protuberances proceeding from the stem, and intended to represent leaves just bursting forth, these are worked in flat satin stitch and spike stitches. The next leaf on the left-hand side is very tastefully devised entirely in bullion stitches, extending in a slanting direction from each margin to the centre of the leaf, where the stitches meet and form a natural mid-rib. The leaf next above this is outlined with very small close overcast stitches, and filled in with diamond pattern filling, with a cross-stitch worked at intervals to secure the threads at the angle of each diamond. On the right-hand side of the spray are two exceedingly pretty leaves worked each in two sections or divisions with stitches of contrasting character ;—the larger leaf has its lower division embroidered in raised

one section is filled with back-stitching in the same manner as the leaf just described, while the other section is tastefully elaborated in rows of small loops of button-hole stitches worked on a thread or "loop" of cotton, in just the same way that the loops are made that are used upon dresses to receive hooks. The pomegranate is outlined with cable-plait stitch (see instructions, page 5, No. 45, of "Weldon's Practical Needlework Series") in two semicircular sections, and surmounted with a tuft worked in button-hole stitches

Three-Sided Brush and Comb Bag. Design of Water Lily and Bulrushes.

satin stitch, slanting from the margin to the centre of the leaf, the stitches being in length graduated to the contour of the leaf, while the upper division is outlined with crewel-stitch, which also is carried as a mid-rib by the side of the satin stitches to form the centre of the leaf, and the entire space between the crewel stitch outline and the mid-rib is occupied with close even lines of small fine back-stitching ; the other leaf is partly outlined with crewel stitch, and

indented from half-an-inch to three-eighths of an inch in height, according to the requirement of the design, and embellished on the top with a row of very tiny French knots. The centre is defined by lines of small fine overcast stitches, and is filled with diamond filling held in place by a bind stitch at the angles, and further ornamented with a small French knot in the middle of each diamond ; then between this centre and the cable plait are two small bars of cable

12

plait on each side. If working a large design, other stitches can be employed for some of the pomegranates, so as to afford a pleasing variety; these can be selected from the preliminary examples issued in No. 45, or will suggest themselves as one gets accustomed to the work. As a rule the more stitches that can conveniently be introduced, and the greater attention that is paid to minute details, the better and handsomer will be the appearance of the work when finished.

PINCUSHION.

CONCH SHELL AND SEAWEED.

THE top of this pincushion is composed of a circular piece of white satin jean, measuring 9 inches in diameter, of which about 6 inches form the covering of the pincushion itself, and is delineated by the level round of crewel stitch that is apparent in the engraving, and the margin thence beyond constitutes a border or frill. A straight strip of jean, 19 inches long and 2 inches wide, is required for the band or side of the cushion, and a circle of calico, 6 inches in diameter, for the bottom; turnings in are not included in this

ornamentation as in the engraving on each side of this line. Th little loops that appear something in the shape of an "O," are com posed of two bullion stitches placed rather closely together, and small space is left between every pair of stitches. The little tin dots on the outer side of the crewel stitch line are in representatio of a double row of small French knots. The scallops are worked i button-hole stitch, and the head of the button-holing is ornamente with eight or nine bullion stitches, each a little distance apart, an in an upward position as shown in the illustration. Knit a sufficien quantity of fringe to go easily round the scallops, or if preferred, a edging of torchon lace may be substituted; but knitted fringe, such as is described at end of description of Nightdress Sachet o page 5, will last as long as the pincushion itself, and is the bes kind of trimming for work of this description.

PRACTICAL SUGGESTIONS
For the Further Development of Mountmellick Embroidery.

THOUGH Mountmellick Embroidery in its modern form is almos

A Swallow.

Spray of Pomegranate.

measurement. A round collar box, measuring 6 inches across the bottom and 2 inches high, will be a capital foundation for making up the shape of the pincushion, which may be stuffed with either bran or wadding.

Trace the design upon the piece of jean with which you intend covering the top of the cushion; the shell must be exactly in the middle, the line for the crewel stitch must be marked to correspond with the exact size of the foundation, and the margin must be outlined with an even number of scallops, and work with Strutt's best knitting cotton, No. 12. Commence with the shell. The outline of this and also the markings of all the "crinkles" on the outside of the shell are worked in cable-plait stitch, and the intervening spaces are filled with bullion stitches on the lower half of the shell, and with bullion stitches and French knots alternately on the upper half. A glance at the illustration will show clearly how this is accomplished. The mouth of the shell is occupied with a series of rows of small button-hole stitches. The sprays of seaweed that surround the shell, as well as the small sprigs of seaweed in the scallops, are worked with the stem of crewel stitch and fronds of bullion knots. Work the circular line of crewel stitch, then do the

exclusively worked according to the instructions contained in the pages of this Work Series, with white knitting cotton upon white satin jean, in which materials it is most particularly suitable for making toilet covers, nightdress sachets, comb and brush bags, pillow shams, quilts, and other domestic appurtenances, which, as a rule, being in constant use, require to be strong and serviceable, it must not be supposed that the work is unsuited to other materials and other purposes; it is, in fact, capable of much development, and there is a growing disposition to employ the Mountmellick stitches upon fine material for table linen, as well as for ornamenting children's little pelisses, frocks, and pinafores, for ladies' fancy aprons, and for the panels and borders of ladies' dresses; and for these purposes either flax thread or embroidery silk would be employed.

It is considered good taste to use nothing but white for table linen; and many leaders of fashion oppose the introduction of colour either in the linen itself or in the embroidery with which the linen is decorated. Certainly white always looks well, and presents a delicacy and elegance peculiar to itself. The introduction of heavy colouring is not to be commended, but lovely tints are now manufactured in Messrs. Harris's flax threads—notably pale blue, pink, old gold, and art greens in every delicate gradation—and remarkable for their fine gloss and brilliancy of finish. These threads are quite well suited for Mountmellick Embroidery upon linen, and may be depended upon for washing perfectly and retaining their glossy appearance. Of course one would not carry out a piece of Mountmellick work in a variety of shades and colours in the style of crewel embroidery, but one shade of flax thread intermingled with white can be made to produce a very pleasing effect.

A dining table-cloth of fine white linen will look very handsome embroidered with a running border of flowers and leaves, or bunches of flowers, or clusters of fruit may be introduced on the corners of the cloth, or small scattered sprays may be powdered lightly over the entire surface. It is customary to have dinner napkins embroidered to correspond.

D'oyleys are usually about 7 inches square, and may have a fruit, or a single flower, or a small spray of flowers in the centre, with a little border of feather stitch, and a fringe of drawn threads; or the centre may be left void and a narrow border be worked round, and the edge finished with a button-hole stitching and a narrow torchon lace.

Large d'oyleys and serviettes are worked with a pretty border, which may be of forget-me-nots, ivy, honeysuckle, or other designs, according to taste.

An elegant sideboard slip is made of white linen or sateen, about 2½ yards long and 14 or 15 inches wide, embroidered with a running border of pomegranates, or oranges, or bulrushes and water-lilies and grasses, with a button-hole stitched edge worked in scallops, and a border of deep torchon lace.

A bread-cloth should be a square or oblong piece of linen, worked with a border of wheat and barley, or other appropriate designs, with a button-hole stitched edge and a border of knitted fringe.

Afternoon tea has become quite a recognised feature in modern society, and the custom has brought tea-cloths and tea-slips into great demand, these therefore present an important and almost unlimited scope for ornamentation. A tea-cloth may be as large as the table requires; a good size for a small occasional table is from 1 yard to 48 inches square; a tea-slip is about 1½ yards long, and 14 or 15 inches wide, and is intended to lay across the head of the table to receive the cups and saucers instead of using a tea-tray. Most of the designs we have illustrated can be turned to account for a bordering, and an arrangement of the "blackberry flowers, berries, and leaves," on page 13, No. 45, will be found very effective and pleasing; the cloth can be finished off with button-hole stitching in scallops, and a lace border, or simply with a fringing of drawn threads. Or the "swallow" page of the present number, might be embroidered in each corner of the cloth, with a trailing design of passion flowers extending half-way along each side. Or a cobweb and spiders with trails of ivy.

Those ladies who like making quilts in patchwork sections will enjoy the idea of preparing a number of squares measuring about eight inches each way, each square being embroidered with a different subject, and the whole sewn together and then prettily feather stitched over the seams; this might be quickly executed after the manner of a "friendship quilt," by a number of friends joining in the enterprise and contributing two or three squares each.

Pillow slips, or pillow shams, may be decorated with little sprigs of flowers dotted about at intervals; or discs, or half-moons, drawn from any good-sized circle, and filled with small flowers in solid work, makes a handsome slip; or a "spread" design after the style of the design of "double marsh marigolds" on the front of the brush and comb bag, page 5, No. 47, might be arranged, and will look very effective made up with a border of knitted fringe.

Children's pelisses and frocks, if of cashmere or soft woollen material, may be effectively embroidered in Mountmellick stitches with Pearsall's embroidery silks or Duncan's washing silks, of shade exactly to match the material; embroidery is rarely now executed with silk of contrasting colour, and it must be owned a self-colour is far the neatest and prettiest. Endless designs for this purpose will be found among Briggs' Transfer patterns, originally prepared for crewel embroidery, but which can well be reproduced in Mountmellick work if only care be taken in selecting such as have a bold, well-defined outline, and plenty of space between the different parts of the design.

Ladies' morning aprons, or work aprons, can be ornamented with a border of Mountmellick work, executed either with flax thread or embroidery silk, according to the material of which the apron is composed.

A flannel dressing-gown, embroidered in a trailing design of "honeysuckle" (see page 13, No. 45) up each side of the front and round the collar and cuffs, will be a great success; and the work is easily accomplished in satin stitch and French knots.

We have seen a lady's bodice made with a yoke embroidered with a honeysuckle design, both bodice and embroidery being one shade of myrtle green, and it looked very pretty and becoming. Many other designs will work out equally well.

A deep border for the bottom of the front breadth of a dress might very tastefully be arranged and worked in Mountmellick Embroidery.

Also the ends of sashes are capable of being embroidered in a dainty manner.

Bands of material or bands of silk may be embroidered separately and put on dresses as an appliqué trimming, either by a neat feather stitching or a couching and spike stitch. A couching consists simply of long strands of cotton, silk, or wool, laid down level with the edge of the band, and fastened at regular intervals by stitches taken across the couching line, then spike stitches are taken at equal distances from each other, from the couched thread over the edge of the band, which thus is held in place.

Many other purposes to which Mountmellick Embroidery can pleasantly and profitably be employed will, doubtless, present themselves to an accomplished worker.

Pincushion.   Conch Shell and Seaweed.

Design of Lilies and Leaves for Mountmellick Embroidery.

Convolvulus and Leaves for Embroidery Purposes.

WELDON'S PRACTICAL
MOUNTMELLICK EMBROIDERY
(FOURTH SERIES).

New and Original Designs for Filling in Leaves, Borders, Edgings, Nightdress Sachet, Tray Cloth, &c.

FOURTEEN ILLUSTRATIONS.

MOUNTMELLICK EMBROIDERY.

Although Mountmellick Embroidery has been so fully treated in previous issues of "Weldon's Practical Needlework Series"—viz., Nos. 45, 47, and 50, price 2d., post free 2½d. each, so many new stitches and designs have been created that we are sure ladies will appreciate our fourth issue, which illustrates some charming ideas for this fashionable and most durable embroidery, as well as a most useful sampler, showing the various ways of working leaves.

EDGING IN DOUBLE HERRINGBONE AND DAISY LOOPS.

A pretty edging can be made with double herringbone stitching and daisy loops, after the style represented in the engraving. This edging is intended for supplementing and widening any border or insertion that is worked in a straight line; and it also may be very usefully applied as an embroidery for underlinen, for which purpose it should be executed with Evan's ingrain crochet cotton or with Harris' flax-thread : of course, for Mountmellick Embroidery the edging will be carried out with the same knitting cotton that is employed for the other portion of the design. Herringbone stitch forms a series of little crosses on the surface of the material; for instruction in working herringbone turn to Fig. 18, No. 45 of

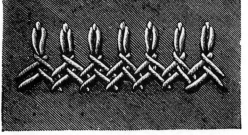

Edging in Double Herringbone and Daisy Loops.

"Weldon's Practical Needlework Series," where the needle is shown in position for taking a stitch ; in the present example the stitches stand about three-eighths of an inch in height, and about one-eighth of an inch of material is taken upon the needle, and rather more than one-eighth of an inch is left open between the stitches. You will probably require a guide for working straight—three or four pencilled lines on the back of the material will answer the purpose, or a succession of small dots may be marked very faintly on the right side, but these should not be at all visible when the work is done. When one row of herringboning has been worked straight along from left to right of the material, a second row is worked in the same manner, taking the stitches a little distance below the stitches of the first row. For the daisy loops—which also are known as leaf-stitch and picot stitch—hold that side of the herringbone

stitching towards you on which you wish the daisy loops to be, and proceed from left to right ; secure the cotton on the wrong side of the material, bring up the needle and cotton to the front level with and in the centre of the first herringbone stitch and draw through, then with the cotton held under the left-hand thumb insert the needle in the same place from which it has just been drawn through, and passing it along the back of the material in a straightforward direction, bring it up a quarter of an inch distance from the herringbone, over the cotton held by the thumb, and draw through, and you have a loop similar to a single chain-stitch loop ; insert the needle a little way beyond this loop to the back of the material and draw through, so making a small straight stitch on the tip of the loop, which, besides being ornamental, serves to hold the loop in place. Thus, every daisy loop consists of two parts, the loop itself, and the short straight stitch on the tip. Work in the same manner, one daisy loop stitch on each herringbone stitch to the end of the row, and the edging will be completed.

BORDER OF MARGUERITES, FLOWERS AND LEAVES.

The handsome wide border here presented to notice measures in the original from 6½ inches to 7 inches wide, and is worked with No. 8 knitting cotton upon white satin jean, in a bold flowing design of marguerites, flowers and leaves. It will suit many tastes, as not being closely nor heavily worked it is quick of execution, and yet at the same time is very effective. The petals of the flowers and also the petals of the buds are executed in highly raised satin stitch, taking the stitches across from side to side of each petal over a padding previously run in ; there are sixteen petals in the full-blown flower, and eight petals in the smaller flower, and eight petals in the buds ; the centres of the flowers are composed of many French knots clustered together in a circle, rather large knots being in the centre and smaller ones outside to produce a spherical appearance ; also the calyx of the buds is simulated by a small group of French knots. The stem consists of many varied stitches, as will be seen by consulting the engraving ; these are ingeniously blended, one running into the other in graceful continuity. You will observe cable-plait stitch, close feather stitch, snail-trail stitch, French knots in double line, and also crewel stitch, and others may be introduced according to the worker's taste and skill. French knots are largely employed for the leaves, because they being all very deeply serrated and indented, the knots lend themselves readily to follow the design, in fact some of the leaves are executed entirely, both outline and veining, in French knots, while in other leaves the cable-plait stitch and the simple feather stitch are used as veining. A pretty leaf on the right-hand side of the border is outlined in a continuation of its stem in snail-trail stitch, the veining being in crewel stitching and bullion stitch. A few intervening leaves are embroidered after the manner of the two leaves at the top of the spray in close feather stitching, and form a good contrast to the open leaves worked in French knots. The design can be repeated and continued to any length desired.

BORDER. POPPIES.

THIS design is intended for a border required to be from 3 inches to 4 inches wide in its actual working. The poppies and the leaves are executed in a very handsome style of Mountmellick Embroidery, using rather fine cotton, say Strutt's No. 10, and working for the most part in neat close stitches. The stem is embroidered entirely in crewel stitch, and curves in a graceful manner to the right and to the left as it runs from the beginning to the end of the border, being sometimes unobservable on account of the flowers and leaves being brought to the front of it. The poppy near the bottom of the stem is represented as full-blown, the petals are outlined with overcast stitch arranged in an almost straight line on the margin, but with a jagged and serrated edge towards the centre of each petal, with slanting stitches down the sides, representing the drooping of the petals; the stamens and pistils are simulated by spike stitches of different lengths surmounted with tiny French knots; a few outline stitches are set in here and there, as shown in the engraving. A bud is formed by two upright petals worked to correspond with the full-blown poppy. Another full-blown poppy, not so large as the first, is embroidered in a similar style, but with the addition of a small broken petal, indicated by a short row of buttonhole stitches. The poppy at the head of the spray is supposed to be half-blown, and consists of three petals, worked much in the same style as the preceding flower. The leaves in this border are most elegant and tasteful in the selection of stitches employed. The first leaf on the right-hand side of the bottom of the stem is beautifully executed in bullion stitches, after the manner of Leaf No. 10 on the sampler, see page 11 of the present issue, and then is finished off with a line of crewel stitch as a mid-rib. The leaf opposite this, to the left of the stem, is outlined with a series of small even buttonhole stitches, and the mid-rib and veining are executed in crewel stitch. Four long

narrow leaves, in representation of blades of grass, appear branching out above the large full-blown poppy; the broadest of these is embroidered in cable-plait stitch, making the stitches tolerably wide in the centre of the leaf and contracting them at the bottom and top; the leaf that curves over the stem is simply outlined all round with crewel stitch, and is elaborated with a row of seed stitch running up the centre; the leaf further to the left is worked in slightly raised satin stitch; and the other small grass leaf has its margin defined with very small overcast stitches, and a line of chain stitch serves as a mid-rib. The other grass leaves that are seen higher up the border are worked in a similar manner to the four leaves just described. The two large handsome leaves almost in the centre of the border will be found in the sampler with full description for working the same. The medium-sized leaf near the top of the spray is very prettily embroidered in two sections; that to the right is outlined with crewel stitch and filled in with numerous dots made in the stitch known as "seed" stitch, and that to the left is worked heavily in raised satin stitch.

The border may easily be continued and repeated for the length required.

BRANCH OF WILD ROSE WITH LEAVES AND BUDS WORKED IN INDIAN FILLING.

THE accompanying engraving demonstrates the use of a stitch known as Indian Filling, which is peculiar to Mountmellick Embroidery, and is seldom if ever applied in a similar manner in any other class of work. It is especially suitable for the working of leaves, and is occasionally used for buds and the petals of flowers. Like crewel stitch, Indian filling is executed almost entirely upon the surface of the material, that is to say, a long stitch is made upon the surface and a short stitch is taken on the under side, and generally the stitches will be somewhat irregular in their length, according to the space that requires filling, as they must adapt themselves to the form of the design. Though a comparatively easy stitch to learn, Indian filling will require careful attention before it can be employed to really good purpose, and proficiency must be attained by practice and patience. the difficulty consists in placing the long stitches so as to lie closely and evenly side by side, each stitch crossing the other and merging one into the other so as to produce the undulating and wavy appearance which is the chief characteristic of this filling, and which our artist has rendered clearly perceptible in the three leaves and also in the buds of the branch of wild rose that is the subject of the present example. The filling may be worked from right to left or from left to right at pleasure.

Border of Marguerites, Flowers and Leaves.

We will suppose you are commencing to learn the stitch, working it from right to left within the space of two horizontal lines drawn half an inch one from the other,—first secure the cotton on the wrong side, then, bring up the needle and cotton to the front of the material on the right-hand side of the lower line, * insert the needle in the upper line straight above the cotton, taking up about one-eighth of an inch of material on the needle and bring out the point straight downwards towards the lower line, being careful to have the cotton to the left of the needle and draw through, insert the needle closely to the left of the stitch just made and one-eighth of an inch above the lower line and bring the point out straight downwards upon the lower line to the left of the previous stitch and with the cotton now to the right of the needle and draw through, and repeat from *; thus the needle is always inserted with its point towards you, and always takes up about one-eighth of an inch of material, and in the first (or top) stitch the cotton is required to be to the left of the needle, and in the second (or lower) stitch it is to be to the right, consequently the second stitch crosses the first; now the surface of the work will appear as if three perpendicular stitches undulated from outline to outline, and the stitches on the wrong side will also stand perpendicularly, but in two neat distinct rows. Practise the stitch in this manner until perfect; then try to work it from left to right; and finally experiment in slanting the stitches as if working a leaf in two divisions with a mid-rib down the centre after the style of the leaves in the engraving.

If you examine the petals of the rose buds, which also are executed in Indian filling, you will notice there is an apparently greater number of undulating stitches; this method is followed whenever you require to fill any rather long space (for instance in filling a large broad leaf), and the procedure is extremely simple,—the first long stitch and the last stitch are always manipulated as instructed above, but one or two additional crossings of the long stitch are made at a convenient interval in the centre of the space by inserting the needle to the left of the long stitch and bringing it out to the right. The calyx of the rose buds is simulated by clusters of very tiny French knots. The centres of the flowers are formed of French knots of rather larger size than those used for the buds; there are five petals to each flower, and each petal is outlined with simple overcast stitch, the widest stitches being along the tip, and slanting stitches down the sides, to make the petals curve gracefully, as represented in the engraving. The stem is throughout worked in crewel stitch.

Several good designs of wild roses are obtainable in Briggs' series of patent transfer papers, notably No. 223, a border of full-blown roses, buds, and leaves, that might easily be adapted for working in Mountmellick Embroidery for a table-cloth or toilet cover, in the style of the branch shown in our engraving and described above.

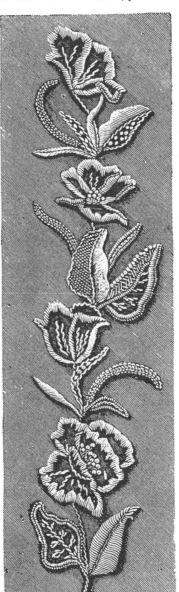

Border. Poppies.

TOILET COVER.

DESIGN OF BLACKBERRIES IN FLOWER, FRUIT, AND LEAVES.

THE original toilet cover from which our engraving is taken affords a splendid example of Mountmellick Embroidery as applied to a most useful purpose and carried out in really effective style. Every one takes pride in having their toilet table elegantly equipped, and this design of blackberries in flower, fruit, and leaves is particularly handsome, and yet not beyond the capability of any fairly experienced worker; in fact, the pattern has been designed on purpose to show the good results that can be attained by the skilful use of the simplest and most generally known stitches Our model cover measures 43 inches wide and 22 inches deep, which is a convenient size for an ordinary table; the front is shaped as represented in the engraving, but this of course is optional, and must depend upon the shape of the dressing-table or chest of drawers on which the cover is to be spread. The foundation is white satin jean, of which 1¼ yards will be required, and the work is executed with Strutt's No. 10 white knitting cotton, and as the knitted fringe consumes a great deal of cotton, you had better procure 1 lb. at once to ensure getting it all exactly the same shade of whiteness. First of all enlarge the design to the size the cover is required to be, drawing it upon a large sheet of tracing paper, or tracing cloth if possible, though a large sheet of strong white paper will answer the purpose just as well, if these are not procurable. Then by the help of transferring paper transfer the design to the material; the method of doing this has already been explained in these columns, see page 4, No. 47, of "Weldon's Practical Needlework Series" (the second issue devoted to Mountmellick Embroidery), and need not be repeated. The margin all round the cloth is worked in scolloped saw-tooth buttonhole stitching, two long stitches and two short stitches taken alternately, as shown in Figure 22, No. 45, of "Weldon's Practical Needlework Series" (the first issue on Mountmellick Embroidery), where will be found complete instructions and illustrations for working all the different stitches to which allusion is made in this description, and also, on page 13, an engraving of a spray of blackberries with flowers and leaves worked in almost natural size, every stitch clear and distinct, and in fact just the very thing for copying into the design now under consideration. If you carefully observe this design you will notice that in every instance the fruit is composed of French knots grouped closely together in a circular cluster, with very highly raised knots in the centre and smaller ones round the outside, in resemblance to the actual berry, as shown in the full-sized example. The flowers also are alike throughout the work, each flower consisting of a centre comprising three small French knots and five petals thickly padded and embroidered longitudinally in closely raised satin stitch. The leaves may be embroidered in many different ways, according to taste. The leaves represented in the full-sized sampler on page 11 are adapted to this toilet cover, and require no special mention except to advise working them as nearly like the example as possible. Many of the leaves are worked solid; a very pretty leaf is outlined with small buttonhole stitches set not too closely together, and filled in with good sized round spots of flat satin stitch in the place of veining; other leaves are executed with a margin of French knots and a filling of trellis stitch; and again a margin of French knots and mid-ribs worked in cable-plait stitch. The stem is delineated by crewel stitch, chain stitch, and cording stitch, and the tendrils by snail-trail stitch. When all the embroidery is finished, the surplus material outside the button-stitched scollops is cut away, and the fringe may be sewn on. The fringe is knitted by the instructions given for knitting the fringe for the nightdress sachet, on page 6 of the present issue, but using only three strands of cotton together to make it less thick.

This design is admirably suited to nightdress cases, brush and comb bags, or may be used as a border for a quilt.

NIGHTDRESS SACHET. DESIGN OF SINGLE DAHLIA.

An elegant and useful nightdress sachet is embroidered in a design of single dahlia flowers, buds, and leaves, as shown in our engraving. It is an interesting piece of work and is almost everlasting wear, and with a comb-bag to match is a possession that any lady will be proud of, whether it be her own work or the gift of a friend. Procure a yard of the best white satin jean, and half a pound or more of Strutt's No. 10 knitting cotton; it does not take a great deal of cotton for the embroidery, but a quantity is used in knitting the fringe, for which a pair of No. 10 or No. 11 steel knitting needles will be required. Divide the satin jean into three pieces, for the front, back, and flap of the sachet; the piece for the front should measure 15½ inches long by 12½ inches deep; that for the back should measure 13 inches long by 11 inches deep; and for the flap, which is worked separately and joined to the top of the back, extending out on each side as far as the front extends, a piece measuring 15½ inches long and 6 inches deep must be allowed. The back of the sachet is not embroidered at all, nor scolloped, but when the sachet is ready for making up it is just simply hemmed with almost invisible stitches upon the front, and entirely within the scollops of the front, which is the reason it is cut so much smaller; it can however, if you like, be cut the same size as the front, and both pieces scolloped together. The front is scolloped round three sides, and the remaining side, forming the top of the bag, is strengthened with a hem. The flap is scolloped to correspond. Commence by tracing the design upon the front and flap as represented in the engraving, including, of course, the scollops and the little seaweed sprays in the scollops, and extending both these latter up to the top of the front underneath the flap. All the full-blown dahlias are worked in resemblance of the natural flower; the seed vessels which compose the centre are simulated by a good-sized oval-shaped cluster of French knots, surrounded in most instances by a circle of crewel stitches, and this again is surrounded by petals, ten or twelve in number, embroidered in the pretty stitch termed Indian filling; see instructions on page 4 of the present issue. A large bud close to the left of the central flower on the front of the sachet is elegantly worked on the one side with a rim of wide closely-set and raised overcast stitches, and on the other and largest side with rows of open button stitching, otherwise called honey-comb, as Figure 32, in No. 45, of "Weldon's Practical Needlework Series;" the tuft on the top of the bud is simulated by a trefoil of close buttonhole stitches, and the calyx is outlined with flat satin stitch combined with a few crewel stitches set in like a veining. Another attractive bud further to the left has both sides outlined with close overcast stitching and its centre filled with honeycomb, and the tuft and calyx the same as the foregoing; and another similar bud will be seen on the top right-hand side of the front; almost directly underneath this latter is a half opened bud of five petals worked in Indian filling from a base of raised satin stitch; and a very small half opened bud on the top left-hand side has three petals worked in satin stitch emerging from a circular calyx of close buttonhole stitch. The broad leaves are defined by an outline of cable-plait stitch, see Figure 8, No. 45, and the centre consists of a mid-rib of crewel stitch extending from the base to nearly the tip of the leaf, with spike stitches branching out at regular intervals on each side, and each spike stitch tipped and finished with a tiny French knot. The long narrow leaves deserve attention, being worked in quite a new style in scollops of rather deep close buttonhole stitches, but instead of these being left in their natural state every three stitches are caught together by a back stitch taken

Branch of Wild Rose, with Leaves and Buds worked in Indian Filling.

right through the material, which has the effect of drawing three stitches together in their centre something like faggots, and also produces a line of dots as shown in the engraving; a row of feather stitching is carried up the centre of the leaf. The stems are variously worked, some in thick overcast stitching, some in chain stitch, and others in crewel stitch, as is clearly apparent in the illustration. The blades of wheat that are introduced here and there among the flowers and leaves are executed in crewel stitch and bullion stitch, as see Fig. 16, in No. 45; and also the seaweed sprays in the scollops are worked in the same way. The buttonholing round the scollops is done over two or three laid threads, in deep close stitches, and therefore being bold and highly raised, has a very pleasing effect. When the Mountmellick Embroidery is all completed, the surplus material is cut away from off the outside of the scollops, and the nightdress sachet can be made up, and trimmed with knitted fringe, as shown in the engraving.

To Knit the Fringe.—You will require to wind a supply of knitting cotton upon four separate balls, and use from all four balls together. Cast on 9 stitches. **1st row**—Make 1 (by passing all four strands of cotton round the needle), knit 2 stitches together, knit 1, repeat this twice. Every row is the same. When a sufficient length is knitted, cast off 5 stitches, draw the cotton through the stitch on the right-hand needle, and break it off; and unravel the remaining 3 stitches for fringe. The fringe is attached by sewing the loop stitches at the top of the heading to the edge of the buttonhole stitches that border the sachet.

MAIDENHAIR FERN.
Worked in Buttonhole Stitch.

Fern leaves are worked in many different ways according to the character of the fern they are intended to represent. For instance, on page 14, No. 45, of "Weldon's Practical Needlework Series," will be seen a spray of ordinary garden fern with its leaves embroidered in flat satin stitch worked smoothly from the outside to the centre of the leaf, some of the stitches being longer than others to mark the serrated edges of the leaf, but joining evenly in the centre to form a line denoting the mid-vein. A maidenhair fern worked in blotches of small close satin stitch is depicted on page 8, No. 47. Another maidenhair fern is prettily executed by means of simple buttonhole stitches, as in the example now illustrated and described; here you will observe the stitches are taken perpendicularly and of almost uniform length from the stem to the top of the frond, extending something in the shape of a fan; a shorter stitch is put here and there to fill in between the long stitches, and the loops of all the stitches come in a row, as in ordinary buttonholing, and make a slight ridge straight along the top of the frond. This method of portraying a fern has a very light and graceful effect. The stem may be embroidered in crewel stitch, snail-trail stitch, or chain stitch, whichever is preferred. Sprays of fern are frequently introduced in combination with flower designs in Mountmellick Embroidery; sometimes they form an essential part of the design and sometimes are employed merely to fill in any small space that would otherwise be left vacant.

SAMPLER SHOWING TWENTY LEAVES WORKED IN THE NEWEST STYLE OF MOUNTMELLICK EMBROIDERY.

The art of producing leaves with taste and skill plays a very important part in the effective execution of Mountmellick Embroidery, and many and various are the stitches that can be brought into use and combined one with another to achieve a satisfactory result; in point of fact, leaves require quite as much thought, attention and elaboration as flowers, and the utmost originality is permissible if combined with good taste. Therefore, in order to render our instructions thoroughly practical and reliable, and because of the difficulty experienced in representing every minute stitch when a complicated design has necessarily to be engraved on a small scale, we have had a sampler prepared on purpose to show twenty leaves, all in the newest and most approved style, in full working size, and with the actual stitches clearly visible, rendering the examples quite easy to copy and work from. The shape of these leaves may, of course, be adapted to the nature of the design the worker is about to undertake; many of them are introduced into certain articles illustrated in this and in previous issues of "Weldon's Practical Needlework Series," as for instance in the tray cloth worked in a design of pomegranates on page 13, the poppy border on page 5 of present issue, and the chrysanthemum border, page 8, and the orange spray, page 9, of issue No. 50. Other leaves and sprays, preliminary stitches in complete detail, as well as handsomely worked articles, such as nightdress cases, comb-bags, toilet cloths, quilt corners, &c., are illustrated in Nos. 45, 47, and 50, of "Weldon's Practical Mountmellick Embroidery," price 2d. each, post free 2½d.

LEAF No. 1. — Taking the leaves in consecutive order as numbered upon the sampler, it will be seen that the outline of the first leaf is defined with crewel stitch, otherwise termed outline stitch and stem stitch, a generally favourite stitch for the purpose because it produces the required result with a small amount of labour; this crewel stitching is bordered on the outside with a line of small French knots, which make a pretty finish to the leaf. The interior of the leaf is filled in with diamond stitch and cross-stitch, executed by first taking long stitches slanting vertically across the leaf from side to side, then crossing these stitches by other long stitches slanting in the opposite direction to form a network of diamonds, and when this is accomplished a simple cross stitch is worked over the threads wherever these cross each other, and thereby the threads are caught down and held securely in their position on the material. The threads of the diamond filling are

Toilet Cover. Design of Blackberries in Flower, Fruit, and Leaves.

not carried across the back of the leaf, for the needle is always set in level with the crewel stitches, and forms two neat rows of stitches on the reverse side of the work.

LEAF No. 2.—In this leaf also the outline is worked in crewel stitch and margined with French knots, but the knots in this instance are rather larger and more prominent than the knots of the first leaf. A mid-rib of crewel stitch passes up the centre of the leaf, and crewel stitch veinings branch out right and left on both sides.

LEAF No. 3.—Here the outline of the leaf is defined by a series of buttonhole stitches worked over two or three strands of cotton laid on the material and held in place until each successive button stitch is in turn accomplished, the stitches being taken quite close one to the other, thus the outline stands rather more raised than it would do by the buttonhole stitching alone. The mid-rib of this leaf is simulated by a line of cable-plait stitch passing in almost a straight direction from the tip to the bottom of the leaf, and on each side of the mid-rib is a decorative line of closely set medium-sized French knots.

LEAF No. 4 is more heavily embroidered than any of the preceding examples and is very effective looking when nicely worked. Begin by running a thread in darning stitch upon the line of the tracing all round the leaf, and work over this in small close overcast stitches, being especially careful to make every stitch as nearly as possible the same size, without drawing the cotton so tightly as to pucker the material; when this is done embroider a line of crewel stitch on each side the overcasting and quite close thereto. For the mid-rib you will require first to lay four strands of cotton upon the surface of the material reaching from the tip to the bottom of the leaf like the strings of a violin; this must be done without any corresponding long threads on the wrong side of the fabric, and you manage it by going to the back only at the top and bottom of the leaf; now cover the long strands with a darning executed in the stitch known to point-lace workers by the term "point de reprise," thus,—having the needle and cotton on the right side of the work take the needle over the first two threads and under the second two threads, and draw through, turn the needle back and pass it over the two threads it just went under and under the two threads it before went over and draw through, and so on darning along the whole length of the leaf, but never taking the needle through the material at all, only over and under the long violin-like threads, and drawing the cotton in easily and not too tightly; there may be three long threads on each side instead of two if you wish a very decided wide ridge of darning. This done, hold the leaf sideways towards you and begin the buttonhole-stitch loops which are made on each side the point de reprise darning in a similar way to the loops made on dresses into which hooks are fastened; you proceed from left to right, bring up the needle and cotton through the material and also through the darning at the extreme verge thereof, insert the needle to the back of the work through the darning and through the material about a quarter of an inch to the right of where it came out and bring it up again in the same place it came out and draw through, and the loop so made, or stitch rather, will retain the darning firmly upon the material; now work a series of buttonhole stitches on the little loop so formed till the loop is full of stitches, and continue working similar loops consecutively till the leaf is finished as represented in the engraving. On the wrong side of the leaf there is in the centre simply a double line of stitches formed by the back thread of the buttonhole-stitched loops.

LEAF No. 5.—This leaf is embroidered in two divisions or sections; work up the mid-rib in crewel stitch, and come down the right-hand side in smooth slanting overcast stitch, keeping the stitches straight upon the outside line of tracing and making some stitches considerably longer than others towards the centre of the leaf to afford

the serrated appearance shown in the example; the other division is filled completely with French knots clustered closely together.

LEAF No. 6 is an elegant leaf worked in two contrasting sections. Run a thread of cotton in darning stitch upon the line of tracing that delineates the left-hand portion or narrowest half of the leaf and overcast this in tiny close stitches of even size, being careful not

Nightdress Sachet

to get the material puckered; this half of the leaf is now to be filled with a series of good-sized crossed stitches, adapting these to the contour of the leaf, so those in the centre of the leaf are rather taller than those at either end, as the space is somewhat wider, and when the row of crossed stitches is so far perfect, re-cross each stitch again where already crossed, so as to form a straight line of small parallel stitches down the centre of the section. The other half of the leaf is first of all thickly and evenly darned from the margin to the centre, and then overlaid in close slanting satin stitch.

Leaf No. 7.—This is a very pretty leaf if skilfully rendered; the outline is worked in the stitch so well known to Mountmellick workers by the name of "cable plait" or "braid" stitch: and the

Design of Single Dahlia.

centre is decorated with five studs or knobs of graduated size, the largest being in the middle; these are executed in flat solid satin stitch, the stitches being taken over and over from side to side in the manner shown in the engraving, and pass, of course, in the same way along on the reverse side of the work.

Leaf No. 8.—Here we see a particularly effective leaf, rendered in two sections in fine close embroidery; the spots depicted on the right-hand section are nothing more nor less than lines of small even back stitching executed with perfect neatness and regularity in rows reaching mostly from the tip to the bottom of the leaf, after the manner of the back stitching that is used in plain needlework, taking up four threads at a time, two threads backwards and two threads forwards to each stitch; the other section of the leaf is a complete contrast, being worked in close slanting satin stitch over a thickly padded foundation.

Leaf No. 9.—The widest division of this novel leaf is worked in raised satin stitch, that is to say, the space within the tracing is filled with numberless darned stitches set thickly in a perpendicular direction from the top to the bottom of the leaf, which darning is afterwards covered with smooth stitches taken slanting from the outside of the leaf to the opposite side of the portion occupied by the darning; the other side of the leaf is outlined with crewel stitch; and intermediately in the space between the crewel stitch and the raised satin stitch the leaf is embellished with a line of pretty dots, or "seeds," as they are sometimes called; to work these the needle is always set in with its point towards you, bring up the needle and cotton somewhere by the tip of the leaf in the position the first seed is required to be, insert the needle two or three threads higher up and bring the point out again where the cotton is and draw through, do this once or twice more, then insert the needle again in the same place and this time bring the point out four or five threads lower than it was brought out before,- as this time it must be in readiness for working another seed, and draw, through, and the first seed is complete; all the other seeds are worked in the same manner, and are about as far distant from one another as the length of the seed itself; the seed stitch is very effective and not at all difficult.

Leaf No. 10.—This is one of the prettiest leaves it is possible to work, and though it takes time to accomplish, the effect when perfect will amply repay any amount of trouble; the stitch employed throughout is the well-known "bullion stitch," otherwise known as "worms;" if you are not acquainted with the stitch you may at once understand how it is executed if you will turn to page 14 of the present issue, where, in the illustration of an "Edging worked in Crewel Stitch and Worms" you will see an example of a worm in process of working, together with instructions for placing the needle, twisting the cotton, and drawing the stitch into position. The bullion stitches in the leaf are worked in exactly the same manner, making them longer or shorter by regulating the number of twists upon the needle, in accordance with the contour of the tracing which shapes the leaf; the stitches are ranged in two rows slanting from the outside to the centre of the leaf, where the junction of the stitches forms a kind of depressed line that serves admirably as a mid-rib, though sometimes the mid-rib is rendered by the addition of a row of crewel stitches running from the stem upwards.

Leaf No. 11.—This charming leaf is most handsomely worked in two contrasting sections, and the small loops on the right-hand side are particularly lacy and pleasing. The section to the left is commenced by first of all outlining the margin with crewel stitch; after which do a row of small neat back stitches straight across the centre of the leaf from the stem to the tip, and continue working back stitch, row after row, till all the space to the outline is well filled; the back stitches are formed by taking up four threads at a time, two threads backwards and two threads forwards to each stitch, the rows get shorter as they approach the outline, as shown in the engraving. Now hold the leaf sideways towards you, and bringing up the needle and cotton close by the stem, begin the button-stitch loops, which are made exactly as the loops made on dresses to pass the hooks into, insert the needle to the back of the work close by the line of back stitch and about a quarter of an inch to the right of the cotton and bring it up again in the same place the cotton springs from and draw through, and work a series of buttonhole stitches on the little loop so formed, until the loop is full of stitches; continue working similar loops consecutively to the tip of the leaf, when fasten off; and begin again on the left-hand side for the commencement of another row, this time arranging for the loops to stretch from the top of one loop to the top of the next loop of the previous row; and proceed in the same manner, rounding the last row of loops to fit into the shape of the leaf, when the leaf will be finished.

LEAF No. 12 is very simple, and yet looks remarkably well in any large piece of work. The outline is embroidered in smooth overcast stitch, and it will be noticed that while the stitches are quite even upon the line of the tracing they vary in length as they slant downwards towards the centre of the leaf, falling into a jagged and serrated edge along the inner margin, in the manner shown in the example. A kind of mid-rib up the centre of the leaf is executed by means of dots, or seed stitches, to work which bring up the needle and cotton towards the top of the leaf in readiness for commencing the first seed, insert the needle about three threads higher up and bring the point out again in the place where the cotton is and draw through, do this twice more, then insert the needle again in the same place and this time bring the point out six or seven threads lower than it was brought out before, as this time it must be in position for working another stitch, and draw through; and repeat the seed stitches equidistant one from the other down the whole length of the leaf.

LEAF No. 13.—Here is a pretty leaf worked in open stitches, and useful as a complete contrast against a leaf of thick and heavy embroidery. Begin upon the mid-rib by running a thread in darning stitch in almost a straight line from the top to the bottom of the leaf, and work over this in small close overcast stitches; come down the left-hand margin of the leaf in seed stitches, taking over two threads only of the material, and set closely one against the other; then work up the right-hand margin in crewel stitch, and you will have the shape of the leaf perfectly outlined. Proceed now to work a few spike stitches branching out from the right-hand side of the mid-rib; and then fill up the space to the left of the mid-rib with a series of tall narrow crossed stitches worked by going first all along from left to right with a slightly slanting stitch on the front of the material and a straight stitch at the back, and then turn and work from right to left, inserting the needle in just the same places, and so making another straight stitch at the back of the fabric alternated with a crossed stitch on the surface, when the crossed threads will appear as they are represented in the engraving.

LEAF No. 14.—This exceedingly pretty leaf is worked in two sections in a novel open style of embroidery. The mid-rib and the outline upon the right-hand side of the leaf are executed in small close overcast stitches over a darned thread that has previously been run in, and now the interior of this section is filled with herringbone stitching taking up not more than two threads of material on the needle on each side close against the overcasting, and placing the stitches quite closely together. The outline on the left-hand side of the leaf is followed in buttonhole stitching, the straight edge of the stitch comes upon the traced line, and the stitches are all about the same length, reaching about a quarter of an inch into the leaf, and placed rather closely together, but not quite touching each other; the narrow space between the buttonhole stitching and the mid-rib is occupied with a row of ornamental cross-stitches, which completes the leaf.

LEAF No. 15.—Here again is an effective arrangement of stitches, some of them rather complicated, but still perfectly easy when once understood, and capable of adjustment in other ways besides the style selected for this very handsome leaf. Commence at the tip of the leaf and proceed in chain stitch down the mid-rib as far as the stem, then turn the leaf to get it in a convenient position to continue the chain stitch upon the left-hand side outline of the leaf to unite again with the chain stitch at the point where this began; the intervening space between the two lines of chain stitches is filled with a series of zigzag stitches embroidered in the similitude of half-diamonds, and a very small seed stitch is worked in the centre of each angle, in the manner shown in the engraving. The other half of the leaf is executed in porcupine stitch and French knots; the porcupine is a long twisted stitch not unlike a spike stitch in appearance but made with a twisted strand of cotton,—bring up the needle and cotton close by the mid-rib a little distance from the top of the leaf, insert the needle in the material just within the tracing on the right-hand side of the leaf and more towards the top, that the stitch when finished may lie in an upward slanting direction, and bring the point out a very short distance from the place the needle was put in and on the direct line of the stitch to the left of the cotton and draw through, pass the needle and cotton from right to left under the porcupine stitch twice or three times, forming a twist, and pass the needle and cotton to the back of the work in the place where the cotton was before brought out and bring it out lower down, close by the mid-rib, in readiness for working another porcupine stitch in the same way; these stitches must all slant in an upward direction; when these are all satisfactorily accomplished a small French knot is worked at the extremity of each, and by keeping the French knots upon the traced line they of themselves form a sufficient outline upon this side of the leaf.

Maidenhair Fern. Worked in Buttonhole Stitch.

LEAF No. 16.—This leaf is formulated in close work imparting a peculiarly rich and distinctive character. The two sections of which it is composed are different in detail, but harmonise well together. The left-hand section is outlined and also the mid-rib is worked in very small fine crewel stitch, and when this is done the intermediate space is filled with slanting lines of intensely neat back stitching. The right-hand section consists of slanting satin stitch raised only very slightly over one layer of darning stitches.

LEAF No 17.—The outline of this pretty open leaf is first of all embroidered in chain stitch; then a line of seed stitch is worked straight down the centre of the leaf in resemblance of a mid-rib, and two lines of seed stitches are utilised as a filling to occupy the open portion of the leaf to the right of the mid-rib and between that and the chain-stitch outline. Also a row of smaller seed stitches is contrived to extend the whole way round the leaf as a pretty finish beyond the crewel-stitch outline. Now, the left-hand open portion of the leaf has to be attended to: you will notice a line of seed stitches lying within the chain-stitch outline, these are worked conjointly with the spike stitches that run into each; bring up the needle and cotton to the front of the work close to the mid-rib and a little way distant from the tip of the leaf, carry the cotton to form a spike stitch running in an upward slanting direction, and insert the needle to take up two threads of the material just within, and level with, the line of chain stitch and draw through, work three stitches one over the other on the two threads of material, and then carry the cotton back in the same direction it came up, and pass the needle and cotton to the reverse side by the mid-rib in just the same place they before came out, and bring up the needle a little way lower down by the side of the mid-rib and draw through; make every stitch in the same manner to the bottom of the leaf, where the spike stitches must be shorter in length as the space grows narrower, and the leaf will be finished.

LEAF No 18.—Commence this leaf in the centre by carrying a line of crewel stitch from the stem to the top of the leaf, and now

Sampler showing Twenty Leaves worked in the Newest Style of Mountmellick Embroidery.

proceed down by the left-hand side of the mid-rib, working a line of rather small seed stitches; the outline on this side of the leaf is delineated by smooth slanting satin stitch, managed so that the stitches come with their even edge upon the outline of the leaf and their jagged edge towards the centre, making the longest stitches long enough to reach nearly to the seed stitches; this is the smallest division of the leaf, as the mid-rib is not in the exact middle, but is a little to the left to give more room for long spike stitches on the opposite side. To make these spike stitches—bring up the needle and cotton close to the mid-rib, about a quarter of an inch or so from the top of the leaf, carry the cotton to run in an upward slanting direction, and insert the needle to take up not more than two threads just within, and level with, the outside line of tracing, and draw through; now carry the cotton again in the same direction, and insert the needle to the back in the same place the cotton before came from, and bring up the needle a little further along by the side of the mid-rib and draw through; continue the spike stitches to the bottom of the leaf; then work French knots upon the traced outline, doing one knot at the extremity of each of the spike stitches, and the leaf will appear as in the engraving.

LEAF No. 19 is a peculiarly attractive leaf, and very handsome, one half being close thick work and the other open. The thick work is executed in satin stitch over a well-padded foundation, and it is kept in a perfectly straight line up the exact centre of the leaf, and branches thence in an upward slanting direction to accommodate itself to the rounded contour of the outline; the stitches, therefore, are longer across the centre of the division than they are at the top or at the bottom. The open work is accomplished in a stitch that will be familiar to lace workers, and practically is a kind of network composed of double buttonhole stitches; hold the leaf sideways towards you and work the first row of stitches as closely as possible against the satin stitch, proceeding from left to right, do two buttonhole stitches quite near to each other, and taking up on the needle not more than about two threads of the material as the stitches must be very small, miss a little space, and then do two more small buttonhole stitches closely together, and continue in the same manner to the end of the row; the next row should be managed backwards, and working two buttonhole stitches on the thread of cotton intermediate between the stitches of last row, and not into the material at all; all the remaining rows are worked as this latter row, going forwards and backwards, and shaping the network to the formation of the leaf; finish by binding the network to the material by a row of crewel stitch worked as an outline over the tracing.

LEAF No. 20.—This leaf is prettily outlined in the effective stitch so well known to Mountmellick workers as cable plait, or otherwise braid stitch; and the centre is filled with a veining of crewel stitches.

BORDER IN CHAIN STITCH, WORMS, FRENCH KNOTS, AND SPIKE STITCH.

THIS attractive little border is useful for many purposes. It consists of a combination of stitches tastefully blended. Two rows of chain stitch extend from left to right along the surface of the material, one at the top and the other at the bottom of the border, and below the bottom row and hanging therefrom are pairs of long "worm" stitches, with their tips surmounted with spike stitches, while between the two rows of chain stitch the work is executed in French knots and spike stitches to the height of five rows, or more or less as required. The bottom row of chain stitch should be worked by the guidance of a proper line of tracing, then any one with a correct eye will be able, by calculating the distances, to bring the border to a satisfactory termination, but, nevertheless, a few parallel lines drawn with a pencil on the wrong side of the material, or a few dots like smocking dots on the right side, will prove a great help in keeping the French knots in regular position

as shown in the engraving. The chain stitch is the kind known as "open" chain, and is worked thus: Bring the needle and cotton to the front of the material upon the traced line, hold the cotton down under the thumb of the left hand, and insert the needle in nearly the same place it came out, but just two or three threads to the right thereof, and passing it along the back of the material, bring up the point towards you about half an inch further upon the traced line, and taking the needle over the cotton held by the thumb, draw the stitch through; again hold the cotton under the left-hand thumb, insert the needle close by the cotton, but immediately outside, and to the right of the stitch just made, and bring it out half an inch further upon the traced line, take it over the cotton held by the thumb, and draw through, and continue, working every stitch in the same manner. The "worms" that embellish the lower side of the chain stitching are worked in pairs, the procedure being the same as instructed for working the edging of crewel stitch and worms (page 14 of the present issue), but in this instance the stitches must be taken in a slanting direction, and almost half an inch in length therefore the cotton will require to be wound fourteen or fifteen times round the needle that the roll may extend nicely over the whole length of the stitch; a couple of spike stitches are added at the extremity of each pair of worms, as will clearly be understood by reference to the engraving. The first line of French knots is worked a very little distance above the line of chain stitching, and the knots are about a quarter of an inch apart one from the other. To make a French knot: Secure the end of the cotton firmly on the wrong side of the material, and then bring the needle and cotton up to the front exactly where you

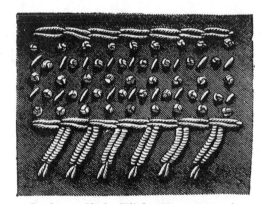

Border in Chain Stitch, Worms, French Knots, and Spike Stitch.

desire the knot to be, hold the needle in the right hand, and while holding the cotton under the thumb of the left hand, twist the needle twice round the cotton in the manner represented in Fig. 28, No. 45, of "Weldon's Practical Needlework Series," and keeping the twist on the needle and with the cotton still compressed under the left-hand thumb, turn the needle round and gradually bring it in an upright position, and put it back in the material a thread or so behind where it came out, and draw the cotton to tighten the knot. The third row of French knots is worked straight above the first row at the distance of about half an inch, and the fifth row again is straight above these; in the second and fourth rows the knots fall intermediate; therefore all the knots are at an equal distance of about a quarter of an inch from each other. The spike stitches are nothing more than simple long stitches lying on the surface of the material between the French knots; they serve as an embellishment and add very much to the good effect of the border when finished. An upper row of open chain stitch will complete the border.

TRAY CLOTH. DESIGN OF POMEGRANATES.

THE illustration represents a tray cloth exquisitely embroidered in a charming design of pomegranates, with the fruit and leaves arranged like a wreath; this is a very favourite subject, and one that works out most effectively. The model cloth is made from a piece of fine quality white satin jean, cut in oval shape, and measuring 27 inches by 18 inches for the extreme outside edge; No. 10 Strutt's best knitting cotton is employed for the Mountmellick Embroidery. The design should be enlarged from the engraving to the size required to fit the piece of material, and when it is properly sketched upon tracing paper, or even upon a large sheet of ordinary paper of any description, it may easily be transferred to the material ready for working. Useful hints upon enlarging and transferring designs will be found on page 4, No. 47, of "Weldon's Practical Needlework Series." The stem of the pomegranate wreath is broad and thick, and therefore is suitably worked throughout in overcasting, taking smooth regular stitches in a slanting direction across from outline to outline; short spike stitches are introduced on each side of the stem to represent the

Tray Cloth. Design of Pomegranates.

[49]

hairy fibre of the natural plant, and these in every case slant upwards towards the top of the stem; and here and there you will observe small protuberances, which are worked in two divisions in flat satin stitch, and surrounded with spikes, to indicate a newly budding leaf. The spray of pomegranate engraved in nearly full working size on page 12, No. 50, of "Weldon's Practical Needlework Series," will be of immense assistance in the correct working of the fruit and also shows five very beautiful leaves, which as illustrated and described there will be recognised in the tray cloth now under consideration, and will be readily understood without further detail. In a few of the pomegranates on the cloth, chain stitch and in others outline stitch is substituted for the rim of cable plait, and in others outline stitch takes the place of the small overcast stitches defining the seed compartment, just for the sake of making a little variety, but the semblance of the fruit is alike throughout as regards the diamond filling and the French knots for seeds and the florescence on the top of the fruit. A remarkable diversity appears in the working of the leaves; indeed, here is a great scope for the imagination, as the greater the variety of stitches introduced the better will be the appearance of the cloth when finished; thus, besides the five leaves referred to above, you will notice the reproduction of many of the leaves from the sampler on page 11 of the present issue, and also several leaves are quite simply worked in feather stitch carried from the margin to the central mid-vein. The tray cloth is finished with small scollops worked in buttonhole stitch, headed by a line of similar scollops worked in cable-plait stitch.

EDGING. CREWEL STITCH AND WORMS.

This little design is intended to be utilised as an edging inside the usual border of buttonhole stitching, which is generally employed as a finish to any article of Mountmellick Embroidery, and it forms a very pretty addition to the same, and will well repay careful working. Though represented in a straight line, the edging is capable of being modified into scollops if desired. A beginner should attain proficiency in working on the straight before attempting curves. Commence by tracing a line upon the material in the place where you wish the row of crewel stitch to be, and work thereon in the usual manner, but taking rather long stitches, that is to say, longer stitches than would be employed if you were outlining a leaf. When the row of crewel stitch is finished, proceed with the "worms," which really are nothing more nor less than "bullion" stitches, arranged after the manner of spikes jutting out from the upper side of the row of crewel stitches. The origin of the term "worms" is lost in mystery, but it is very generally adopted by Mountmellick workers as a designation for this particular stitch, and certainly is very appropriate, although not nearly so euphonious as the time-worn appellations of "twisted stitch" or "bullion," "roll picot" or "point de minute," all different names for the same stitch. To work,—bring up the needle and cotton close to the upper side of a crewel stitch, insert the needle at a distance of about half an inch or three-eighths of an inch above the line of crewel stitching in the direction you wish the "worm" to lie when finished, and passing it along the back of the material, bring out the point in the place the cotton springs from, and now carefully and evenly wind the cotton eight or nine times closely round the needle with the right hand, while you hold the needle steadily in position by pressure of the left-hand thumb, and the needle and cotton will now be in the position shown in the engraving; thus you will see the length of the stitch is regulated by the amount of material taken on the needle, which is equivalent to the length the "worm" will be when finished; keep the left-hand thumb pressing firmly on the roll of stitches while you draw the needle and cotton through the material and also through the roll of stitches, then gently pull the cotton upwards till the

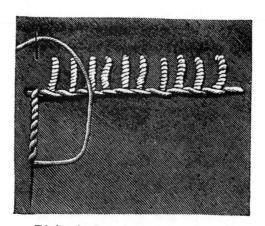

Edging in Crewel Stitch and Worms.

"worm" lies smoothly on the surface of the material, when pass the needle to the back of the work where it was before put in at the top of the stitch, and bring it to the front again by the line of crewel stitching in readiness for commencing the next stitch. All the "worm" stitches are manipulated in this manner. It is no consequence whether you work from right to left or from left to right, the important thing is to retain the left-hand thumb firmly pressing upon the roll of stitches until the cotton is quite drawn through; if the roll is released too soon it will fall out of place and be almost impossible to get it evenly together again. If done rightly, the roll will lie compactly in its intended position on the material. Experienced embroiderers will, of course, comprehend this stitch by the engraving without requiring to follow any explanation. We advise novices to practise until perfect, as it is a stitch that is employed more or less in almost every piece of Mountmellick Embroidery, and always looks effective.

On page 7 of No. 45 of "Weldon's Practical Needlework Series," price 2d., post free 2½d., and which forms the 1st Series of Mountmellick work, will be seen worm or bullion stitch arranged in sprays, and it is effective for representing wheat-ears, for the veining and centre of leaves, &c.

Other useful stitches illustrated and fully detailed in the same issue are crewel or outline, overcasting, chain stitch, cording, snail trail, cable, double cable, cable plait, single coral, double coral, single, double and treble feather, herring-bone, wheat-ear, buttonhole stitches; saw tooth, indented, scolloped, and fringed buttonholings; French knots, couching, back stitch, honeycomb, bullion, loop, brick, and diamond stitches for filling in, also various ways of working leaves; spider web; loop stitch, and cog wheel rings, knitted fringe, and lovely sprays of honeysuckle, blackberries and leaves, branch of hops, spray of ferns, and a nightdress case worked in passion flowers and asters.

No. 45 of this series details everything in connection with Mountmellick Embroidery, and will be of the greatest assistance to amateurs, while those proficient in this delightful embroidery can gain many hints as to how to group various flowers and stitches to best advantage. No. 47, the second series of Mountmellick Embroidery, gives charming designs for toilet mats, toilet covers, brush bags, spray of fuchsia, ivy leaves, white lilies, oak apples and leaves, wheat, barley and grass, forget-me-nots, fern sprays, pansies, &c.

WELDON'S PRACTICAL
MOUNTMELLICK EMBROIDERY

(FIFTH SERIES).

New and Original Designs for Pillow Sham, Comb-Bag, Borders, Toilet Cover, Nightdress Sachets, D'Oyleys, &c.

SIXTEEN ILLUSTRATIONS.

MOUNTMELLICK EMBROIDERY.

WE think our readers will be pleased to see another issue treating of Mountmellick Embroidery, and therefore we now publish our fifth series, containing many charming and valuable designs for this favourite work, which still retains its popularity, and, in fact, is never likely to sink into oblivion; it is so useful, so durable, and such handsome results can be produced for a trifling expense. For preliminary instructions in Mountmellick Embroidery, workers should possess themselves of No. 45, No. 47, No. 50, and No. 69 of "Weldon's Practical Needlework Series," price 2d., or post free 2½d. each. These are illustrated with an immense variety of stitches, examples, and fully worked designs, all of which are accompanied with clear and explicit instructions for working.

A NEW KNITTED FRINGE FOR TRIMMING MOUNTMELLICK EMBROIDERY.

THIS fringe is useful for trimming toilet sets and other articles of Mountmellick Embroidery for which a lighter and more open fringe is desired than the ordinary handsome thick, crinkly fringe that has already been described in these columns, see illustrations and instructions pages 12 and 13, No. 45, and page 5, No. 50, "Weldon's Practical Needlework Series." It may be worked with either single or double cotton; single cotton is employed for the example shown in the engraving, but if the fringe is preferred thicker, the cotton may be double, that is, wound in two separate balls, and knit from the two balls together. Procure two skeins of Strutt's best knitting cotton, No. 6 or No. 8, and a pair of No. 11 or No. 12 steel knitting needles, also a bone netting mesh from 1½ inch to 2 inches wide to determine the depth of the fringe, or if a netting mesh is not handy, a strip of very thick cardboard will answer equally well. Begin by casting on 7 stitches. **1st row.**—Insert the needle in the first stitch in the usual manner, take the mesh and hold it between the thumb and first finger of the left hand close up to the work, and pass the cotton first along the back, and then up the front of the mesh, and round the point of the right-hand needle, and knit off the stitch, keeping it close to the mesh on which the loop of fringe is wound, knit plain the next stitch, make 1, knit 2 together, make 1, knit 2 together, knit 1. **2nd row.**—Slip the first stitch, knit 6. Repeat these two rows alternately for the length required. When the mesh gets full of loops, those at the end can be slipped off to make room for more. A twist is given to each loop by putting in a knitting pin and twisting the strands of cotton tightly one over the other, then draw the pin out, and the fringe will appear as in the engraving.

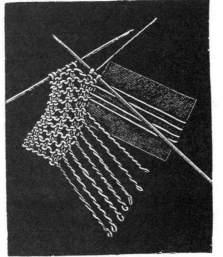

A New Knitted Fringe for Trimming Mountmellick Embroidery.

CHAIN-STITCH TRELLIS.

DESIGN FOR FILLING-IN.

THIS is engraved in the actual working size, and is a very effective design for filling-in; it covers the surface of the material with an open diamond lattice of chain stitch, and may be employed equally well for filling large or small spaces, as if the space is small the trellis can be reduced accordingly. The dot that appears in the centre of every open diamond is formed by working two or three back stitches, or dot stitches, one over the other. The method of embroidering simple chain stitch is illustrated and explained on page 4, No. 45, of "Weldon's Practical Needlework Series," and is familiar to all fancy workers. In the present example every line is commenced at the top, and worked downwards, slanting vertically to the right till all the lines in that direction are accomplished, and then in the same way working lines to slant to the left and cross over the first; and when the trellis is complete the dots are manipulated as shown in the engraving, or a French knot may be inserted in the centre of each diamond if preferred to the dot stitch.

WIDE INSERTION FOR A SIDEBOARD CLOTH.

THE insertion shown in our engraving is a floral subject conventionally treated, and is suitable for working down the centre of a sideboard cloth, or along both sides, whichever is desired; of course if it be worked on both sides the labour is doubled, but the cloth is much more handsome. Procure a strip of white satin jean about 2 yards long and 18 inches wide, and trace the design thereon. Use Strutt's No. 10 best knitting cotton for the embroidery. The complete insertion is 6½ inches wide; and ¾ of an inch on each side is devoted to the marginal edge, leaving 5 inches for the floral device. First define the margin by working two parallel lines of cable-plait stitch on each side the insertion, and between these lines embroider a little running scroll in simple crewel stitch. The floral portion of the insertion is executed in an immense variety of stitches, and though not presenting much difficulty to those who have mastered the instructions given in previous numbers of this work series, is yet an elaborate task, requiring both skill and attention. If you carefully observe the engraving you will first of all notice the gracefully curved stem which is entirely executed in cable-plait stitch, otherwise called braid stitch, one of the prettiest stitches peculiar to Mountmellick Embroidery, and explained in detail on page 5, No. 45. A large tulip-shaped flower consisting of three sectional compartments, each outlined with crewel stitch, will next command attention; the central compartment is occupied with a pretty open diamond lattice worked in neat chain stitch after the manner of chain-stitch trellis just described, but much smaller and closer and minus the dots, while the two side compartments have slanting bar lines running latitudinally across them and French knots dotted between the lines; on one side the bar lines are formed of long loose chain stitches and on the other side of a couple of strands of cotton couched down together; the tops of two petals worked in smooth satin stitch appear to be bursting as it were from the inside of the top of the flower. A smaller flower, or bud, on the opposite side of the main stem, is most daintily realised by a skilful arrangement of stitches, thus, two of the four petals are embroidered in slightly

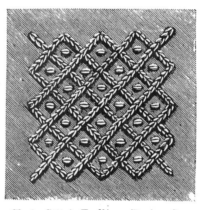

Chain-Stitch Trellis. Design for Filling-in.

Wide Insertion for a Sideboard Cloth.

stitch, its point folded under, and its centre decorated with a mid-rib of satin-stitch spots. A large leaf, or rather spray of leaves, is edged with moderately wide overcasting, and veined respectively with diamond filling, crewel stitch, snail-trail stitch, feather stitch, and coral stitch, as will be seen in the engraving. A thin long leaf branching upwards from the main stem is outlined with neat back stitching and filled with honeycomb network as far as the upper portion of the leaf is visible, and where it folds under the network is changed to two parallel lines of crewel stitch. The next leaf to this is also long and thin, the outline is crewel stitched, and a very pretty mid-rib is worked in "point de reprise" and button-stitch loops, which will be best understood by referring to leaf 4 on the sampler of leaves, page 11, No. 69, "Weldon's Practical Needlework Series." A small leaf lying immediately below on the opposite side of the stem is outlined with chain stitch and crossed obliquely with blotches or bars of raised satin stitch; the next leaf is composed of buttonhole stitches of graduated length, the stitches meeting and forming a natural mid-rib down the centre of the leaf. A group of three leaves a little to the left deserves notice on account of the beauty of the stitches used in filling; they are all similarly outlined with crewel stitch, the middle leaf is filled with Brussels net stitch, to effect which first take long stitches across the surface from one side of the leaf to the other side in an oblique direction, cross these with other long stitches from side to side slanting in the opposite direction and forming diamonds, then lengthways of the leaf but diagonally take three or four long stitches in "darning" fashion, passing the needle alternately over and under the threads of the diamonds; the other two leaves are embroidered with the lace stitch known as "pyramid" stitch, which really is a series of little satin-stitch triangles; the first satin stitch (beginning at the base of the leaf) will form the bottom of a triangle, and each successive stitch is a trifle shorter on each side until the top is reached, where a very small stitch no larger than a dot stitch is required to complete the triangle; these must be kept regular in size, fitting nicely one against the other, and the smaller they are the more "lacy" will be the effect. A pretty neat leaf to the right of the flower bud is outlined with a

raised satin stitch; the petal between these forms a contrast being outlined with crewel stitch and crossed and recrossed with threads of cotton in diamond fashion; wherever the threads cross each other they are held in place by a tiny cross-stitch, and the interstices of the diamonds are each occupied with a very small French knot; the remaining petal is margined with crewel stitch and filled with minute back stitches placed irregularly but closely together; three stamens represented by cord stitch emerge from the flower and are tipped by small anthers of raised satin stitch. The leaves are remarkable for their variety, scarcely any two being alike. A long slender leaf to the right of the design is outlined with cable

double margin of crewel stitch, between which is set a line of tiny French knots.

Another leaf is executed entirely in bullion stitch, and another in Indian filling; the method of working these has already been described in these columns. A leaf outlined in the usual manner with crewel stitch is elegantly filled with cross-stitches and French knots; take long stitches straight across the surface from side to side of the leaf and at short regular intervals one from the other, when these are done put one cross-stitch in the middle of each space from the base to the tip of the leaf, and up each side of the leaf midway between the cross stitches and the outline put a tiny French knot.

The tendrils that appear in various parts of the design are rendered in snail-trail stitch. This is really a most interesting piece of work owing to the diversity of the stitches.

BORDER AND CORNER FOR A TABLE-CLOTH, TOILET COVER, OR QUILT.

Scroll patterns are nearly always effective and pleasing. The one selected for our engraving makes a particularly handsome border for a small table-cloth, a toilet cover, or a quilt, as the curves are bold and striking and the design throughout is strictly in accordance with good taste. The original border is 4 inches wide, and is worked with No. 12 knitting cotton on white satin

represented by an outline of small closely worked buttonhole stitches, with a few feather stitches to simulate a veining. The plume in the other bend of the scroll comprises five petals embroidered in raised Indian filling spread above and around a centre that is buttonhole-stitched and filled to correspond with one of the petals of the buttercup before mentioned, the plume rests on a pair of anthers worked thickly in raised satin stitch, and a spray worked in leaf stitch hangs gracefully below. The large medallion in the corner has a centre of French knots placed thickly in a circle, and surrounded with eight petals similar to those used in the buttercups, and these again are surrounded with eight larger petals embroidered in highly raised satin stitch and separated one from the other by eight thick bullion stitches which for the sake of effect are worked with No. 6 cotton and are quite an inch in length. The ornament that rises above the inside corner of the scroll consists of

Border and Corner for a Table-Cloth, Toilet Cover, or Quilt.

jean; the fringe surrounding the cloth is knitted with No. 8 cotton. The border may be enlarged to the width of 6, 7, or 8 inches, in which case it will be better to use No. 6 cotton for the embroidery and for the fringe also.

The scroll is formed primarily of two curved lines, and great care must be taken in the tracing to get the curves very true and exact, and the lines always just the same distance one from the other, for any grave inaccuracy will spoil the appearance of the work when finished. The thicker of the two lines is executed in cable-plait stitch; the other line, the one that is gradually brought to a peak in the centre of the upward bends of the scroll, is feather-stitched. The enclosures formed by the line of feather stitching are filled with a medallion somewhat resembling a buttercup, the centre of which is composed of a ball of raised satin stitch, and the four petals being

a star of raised satin stitch combined with leaf-stitch sprays. All these details being attended to there remains but to add the drops or pendants that hang from the lower edge of the line of cable-plait stitching; of these there are seven on each bend of the scroll and twenty-one round the corner; they are made by working four or five snail-trail stitches for the length of the pendant and dotting the end with four small French knots.

We have already supplied instructions for making the **Knitted Fringe** that is so generally used for bordering articles worked in Mountmellick Embroidery, see page 6, No. 69, for a fringe of nine stitches wide, page 5, No. 50, for a fringe of twelve stitches wide, and page 12, No. 45, of "Welden's Practical Needlework Series," for an engraving in full working size. In old times it was the custom to *purl* the stitches instead of knitting them, and some people even now think that by this means a more twisted-looking heading is produced, but the difference is very slight indeed, and if anything the purling process takes longer time to accomplish; however, if any one likes to try the experiment, here is the formula. Cast on 9 stitches in the usual way—that is, having the cotton wound in three or in four separate balls, and using from all the balls together. **1st row**—Pass the cotton quite round the needle to make a stitch, purl 2 stitches together, purl 1; make 1, purl 2 together, purl 1; make 1, purl 2 together, purl 1. Every row is alike. When a piece of sufficient length is accomplished, cast off 5 stitches, draw the cotton through the stitch on the right-hand needle and break it off; and unravel the remaining stitches to form the fringe.

NIGHTDRESS CASE.
DESIGN OF PASSION FLOWERS.

AN attractive design of passion flowers in various stages of

unnecessary. There is on the nightdress case a thick stem running across from side to side both on the pocket and on the flap, this is embroidered with Strutt's No. 6 knitting cotton in the stitch known as cable plait, for detail of which turn to page 5, No. 45, "Weldon's Practical Needlework Series;" the flowers and leaves and tendrils are executed with No. 8 cotton, which is a size finer than No. 6: it will be seen that while some of the passion flowers have stamens rising within the arc or corona of bullion stitches after the manner of the previous instructions, other flowers are filled more simply by five or six French knots. The stems appertaining to the flowers and the leaves are severally worked in crewel stitch, chain stitch, and cord stitch; the tendrils are in snail-trail stitch; and the sprays of small feathery leaves are a replica of the example Fig. 45, No. 45. A few of the large leaves are embroidered in smooth satin stitch; others are outlined with small French knots and filled with feather-stitch veining; a pretty leaf on the right-hand side of the pocket and also another on the flap are defined with crewel stitch with a

Nightdress Case.   Design of Passion Flowers.

development with leaves and tendrils in sufficient luxuriance to produce a good effect without too much overcrowding the surface of the material; it is a subject that an amateur may take up and carry out in really effective style, for passion flowers lend themselves well to the stitches used in Mountmellick Embroidery, and they are in fact one of the most favourite flowers in vogue for this style of work, while a pretty nightdress case with a comb-bag to match is always esteemed for a present if not destined by the worker for her own use.

Our model nightdress case is 17 inches long and 11 inches deep, the flap is 3½ inches deep; it is made of white satin jean of the best quality, and on this the design is traced in the usual manner, see instructions page 4, No. 47, "Weldon's Practical Needlework Series," in which issue also will be found, on page 12, a branch of passion flowers and leaves in almost full working size with the stitches so clearly illustrated as to almost render a verbal explanation

line of French knots running as a mid-rib up each section. The nightdress case is edged with fringed buttonholing worked with No. 6 cotton; several threads of padding are first of all to be run above the outline of the scollops so that the buttonhole stitches may be highly raised; then having provided yourself with a flat bone mesh measuring about an inch wide to regulate the size of the loops of fringe, bring up the needle and cotton in readiness on the outside of the scollop, and working from left to right do one plain buttonhole-stitch over the padded threads, take the mesh between the thumb and first finger of the left hand and holding it close to the outline bring the cotton first over and then under the mesh, insert the needle above the padded threads and bring it up on the outline as near as possible to the right of the previous stitch and with the cotton to the right of the needle, and draw the needle and cotton through, next do a plain buttonhole-stitch, then a fringed button-hole-stitch, and so on alternately, taking the stitches as closely together as possible that the fringe may be thick and the padding well covered; as the mesh gets full it can be drawn away to accommodate more loops of fringe; take pains to preserve the scollops in good shape and all equal in size; the fringed buttonholing along top of nightdress case is worked in a perfectly straight line.

PILLOW SHAM. OWL ON IVY.

THIS is a quaint design, especially suitable for Mountmellick Embroidery, and very effective. The flowers are treated conventionally, and the owl, in highly raised work, looks very clever sitting on veining. The next two leaves are outlined in a similar manner, but are veined with snail-trail stitch. Two leaves, still higher up the stem, are worked also in the same way. Two small leaves, nearly at the top of the spray, are outlined with snail-trail stitch, and filled in with French knots; and the two remaining leaves are worked as the two first. The bud at the top of the spray is very beautifully fashioned in long bullion stitches, or as they are often called, "worm" stitches, every three or four of which combine together as it were to form a little fold overlapping the bud, and overlapping each other. The half-opened honeysuckle is executed in highly raised overcasting; and the same stitch is employed for the full-blown flower, excepting on the tips of the curved petals, where the stitch

Pillow Sham.   Owl on Ivy.

the spray of ivy. Procure a piece of white satin jean the size you desire your pillow sham to be, the one from which the engraving is taken is 26 inches by 17 inches; you also will require about half a pound of Strutt's No. 8 knitting cotton, and a skein or two of No. 12. The spray, to the right of the pillow sham, consists of honeysuckle flowers and leaves; use No. 12 cotton, and for the main stem work a double line of snail-trail stitch as shown in the illustration, with French knots running straight between the lines of snail-trail stitch all through the upper portion of the stem, and thickly studded where the stem at the base is thicker. Two leaves, very near the bottom of the stem, are outlined closely with cable-plait stitch, and simply veined in the ordinary way with crewel-stitch

changes into buttonholing. A little Indian filling is introduced over the middle petal, from which stamens project upwards. All the stamens are composed of crewel stitch, and a cluster of thick French knots represents the seed vessel at the base of the flower. All the tendrils on this spray are executed in snail-trail stitch. The other spray, lying on the left-hand corner of the pillow sham, consists of a small bough of oak, with oak apples and grasses. The grasses are embroidered lightly in snail-trail stitch, the tallest sprig is worked in leaf stitch, and the other with bullion stitches. The oak leaves are elegantly produced in Indian filling, with a mid-rib of crewel stitch; the margin of the leaves is deeply serrated. The four oak apples are represented in the form of a circle or ring, very thickly padded, and thickly covered with buttonhole stitch. Four of the apples have their centres filled with very small French knots, and the other has a diamond filling, produced by sewing single threads across and across from side to side, forming a trellis-like network.

The stem of the **ivy-leaf spray**, in the centre of the pillow sham, is embroidered partly in crewel stitch and partly in cable plait; the four ivy leaves are simply outlined with snail-trail stitch, two of them have a filling of crewel-stitch veining, and the other two are veined with French knots. The **owl** is first of all to be back-stitched throughout the entire outline, then pad the legs thickly, overcast them, and make three or four small worm stitches to simulate claws. Next add the tail, which consists of long worm stitches, and long twisted stitches placed alternately. The body must now be firmly stuffed by sewing it over and over till it gets a fair thickness, when, having the needle threaded with No. 8 cotton double, pass the needle up and down, making the stitches lie as if they were feathers, or as if you were shading the owl with a pencil. The wing is partly executed in much-raised satin stitch, working " in shape," and simulating the tail feathers with very long bullion stitches; and partly (this towards the top of the wing) stuffed to match the body, and covered like the body with stitches lying like feathers. The head is padded even to a greater thickness than the body part, and it then is worked over in a similar manner, keeping the hollow for the eyes, and piling stitches upon stitches till a satisfactory head is attained. For the feathers round the eyes, cut a few lengths of cotton, about $\frac{1}{4}$ inch long, and stitch them firmly in position in such a way as to make the ends stand upright, then having filled the space, and being careful to leave the openings for the eyes quite clear, trim it neatly into shape with a sharp pair of scissors; put in a French knot for each eye; and for the beak place a few threads as a foundation on which to work a few point-de-reprise stitches, or let the beak consist of a bullion stitch. To embroider this owl properly, it must be borne in mind that the stitches must be placed exactly as the feathers would lie on the bird. Making a trial will elucidate the matter quicker than any verbal explanation.

The pillow sham is bordered with scollops of indented buttonhole-stitch, worked as instructed, Fig. 25, No. 45, of "Weldon's Practical Needlework Series." It is then trimmed with knitted fringe.

and yet presenting no special difficulty of execution, as there is no overcrowding in any part of the pattern and only the best-known stitches are brought into requisition. The engraving does full justice to the work, it is so clear and distinct, and shows every detail most accurately.

The toilet cover from which the engraving is taken measures 44 inches wide by 26 inches deep, and is handsomely finished off with

Toilet Cover.

TOILET COVER.

DESIGN OF LEMONS.

A MOST original and beautiful design has been prepared for a toilet cover, and is here presented to our readers. The subject is **Lemons**, combined with small lemon flowers and leaves, and the whole most effectively grouped together in such a manner as to form a border running along the front and up the sides of the cloth. It is a really splendid piece of work, very bold and important looking,

scolloped buttonholing and knitted crinkly fringe. White satin jean is the material employed for the foundation, and the work is executed with Strutt's knitting cotton No. 8 and 10, the former for the stem, the leaves, the buttonholing, and the fringe, and the latter for the other portions of the design.

The first proceeding is naturally to enlarge the design from the engraving to the actual size of the toilet cover, and the next to trace it upon the material; full instructions for both these processes will be found on page 4, No 47, of "Weldon's Practical Needlework Series" (the second issue devoted to Mountmellick Embroidery). The working of the stem next demands attention; it is embroidered throughout, both the main stem and the minor ones, in cable-plait stitch, a particularly suitable stitch for the purpose, as it is perfectly

...esign of Lemons.

smooth and flat and lends itself easily to be widened or narrowed at pleasure. The lemons are composed entirely of French knots, mostly large in size, especially those in the central part of the lemons, but becoming smaller as they approach the outline, so giving the fruit a finely raised spherical appearance. The flowers very much resemble the familiar blackberry flower; they consist of five petals

grouped round a centre of five or six very small French knots, the petals being embroidered lengthways in highly raised satin stitch. The leaves are mostly long and rather narrow in shape, a good many are worked in flat feather stitch in the same way as the leaf shown in the illustration Fig. 40, No. 45, "Weldon's Practical Needlework Series," but with an even edge; other leaves are outlined with French knots, a mid-rib of crewel stitch is carried up the centre, and bullion stitches spring out on each side therefrom; another and similar mode of working is to outline the leaf with French knots and put in a veining of trellis stitch, or a filling of honeycomb, or open diamond work; yet another style of leaf has the margin embroidered with small buttonhole stitches, and a mid-rib of medium-sized French knots. A great variety of stitches may be brought into the leaves by an ingenious worker; the sampler on page 11, No. 69, will afford many valuable suggestions, representing as it does no fewer than twenty leaves in real actual size. When the whole of the embroidery is finished the edge of the material is worked in indented buttonhole-stitch in scollops, from which the outer margin is afterwards cut away. It is then trimmed with fringe knitted for the purpose, instructions for which appear on page 6, No. 69, and also at end of description of Border and Corner for a Table-Cloth in present issue.

D'OYLEY. FIELD DAFFODILS.

THE design is a wreath of field daffodils, and the work is executed with Strutt's No. 16 knitting cotton upon fine white twilled linen. The work is exceedingly close and fine, almost as fine as Swiss embroidery. The d'oyley is 8½ inches in diameter; the edge is buttonhole-stitched in small scollops, and a narrow torchon lace is sewn on with fulness. As the stem of the wreath is rather thick and massive it is appropriately embroidered in raised overcasting, that is, two or three darning threads are run within the outline, and then are covered with overcasting, working firmly, and avoiding to pucker the material. The daffodil flower consists of a cup and five petals, the top of the cup is defined by working a small circle in crewel stitch, the cup itself is composed of flat satin stitch worked longitudinally from the bottom to the top of the cup by the circle of crewel stitch; the petals are embroidered after the manner of little leaves, working in slightly raised satin stitch from the outside margin to the centre, where the stitches meet and form a natural vein, or what, if it were a leaf, would be termed a mid-rib. Every flower is embroidered in the same manner. The buds are very similarly worked, only they are smaller, and the petals cling round close up to the cup in the manner shown in the engraving. The leaves are long, thin, and tapering, and many of them are half folded back as if blown by the wind. Some of the leaves will be recognised as being similar in detail to leaves that are included in sampler on page 11, No. 69, "Weldon's Practical Needlework Series."

A singularly pretty leaf is embroidered in uneven sections of close and open embroidery ; the close work, which occupies the left-hand side of the leaf, is done in moderately raised satin stitch, the open work is executed by means of a row of long twisted spike stitches that emerge from the centre of the leaf and branch out to the tracing, which on this side is dotted with a line of French knots, one knot being on the extremity of every spike stitch. Another elegant leaf has its outline clearly defined with small close overcast stitches, and the intermediate space is occupied by a few open and rather wide cross-stitches as will be understood by reference to the illustration ; then, when the cross-stitches are fully worked, an extra stitch is passed lengthways over the crossed threads. A very effective leaf is represented as being outlined with crewel stitch, the upper portion is then closely filled with rows of very tiny back stitching, and the lower portion, which apparently is turned or folded over as if bent, is worked in smooth satin stitch across from outline to outline. The

A comb-bag of very similar shape embroidered in a design of double marsh marigolds appears on page 5, No. 47; and a very handsome three-sided bag worked in raised bulrushes and water-lilies will be found on page 11, No. 50, "Weldon's Practical Needlework Series."

D'OYLEY. MOUNTAIN ASH.

WORKED in a design of mountain ash berries and leaves grouped in a wreath, a favourite subject, and one that always looks light and elegant from its very simplicity. The foundation of the d'oyley is a piece of fine white twilled linen, on which the embroidery is worked with Strutt's No. 16 knitting cotton ; the model measures 8¼ inches across from side to side, not including the lace edging. You will notice that the wreath is apparently formed of a number of small

D'Oyley. Field Daffodils.

remainder of the leaves, which all are very thin and narrow, are either so plainly engraved as to be clearly copied without verbal instruction, or else are included in the sampler to which reference has been already made.

COMB-BAG.

DESIGN OF PASSION FLOWERS.

THIS is intended to accompany the nightdress case illustrated on page 6 ; a yard of white satin jean will be more than sufficient to make the pair, and any that is left over can be used for toilet mats to match. The comb-bag measures 12 inches long by 9 inches wide, the flap is 3½ inches deep. The design corresponds with the design on the nightdress case, and the working of the flowers, leaves, and other details will be understood by turning to the instructions thereof.

detached branches overlapping each other, and each branch has its own particular spray of leaves all worked in the same manner; the sprays, however, differ very considerably one from the other in the mode of embroidering the leaves, innumerable stitches being employed, and the result is that no two sprays are alike. The stem throughout the wreath is worked in crewel stitch. A particularly pretty spray of leaves is executed in very fine close bullion stitches lying slanting from the outside to the centre of the leaf, where the junction of the stitches forms a kind of natural mid-rib; this leaf is represented by No. 10 in the sampler on page 11, No. 69, "Weldon's Practical Needlework Series." Another effective spray of leaves is worked with an outline of small close buttonhole stitches and a mid-rib and veining of crewel stitch. In one charming spray all the leaves are worked in two sections, the section on the left-hand side is raised satin stitch, and the section on the right, to form a contrast, is filled in closely with rows of small back-stitches, like leaf No. 8 in the sampler. Another spray has its leaves outlined with seed stitch and filled in the interior with trellis stitch. A simple spray of leaves is worked in close feather stitch. And yet in another spray the leaves resemble leaf 2 in the sampler. The mountain ash berries hang in clusters dependent from stems of fine crewel-stitch, and are worked as highly raised as it is possible for such small berries to be, a few small close stitches of padding are put in, and these are covered longitudinally with satin stitch, and on the tip of each berry is one tiny over-laid stitch, a mere spot, to represent the speck in the top of each natural ash berry. The Mountmellick Embroidery is all very close and fine, in fact almost as fine as Swiss embroidery, or so much could not be compressed in the allotted space : if the design were required to be worked with No. 8 cotton upon a foundation of satin jean it could be enlarged and rendered suitable for a tray-cloth or other purpose. The margin of the d'oyley is worked in small scollops of buttonhole stitching, and an edging of torchon lace is fulled round, and completes the d'oyley.

NIGHTDRESS SACHET.

DESIGN OF HOPS AND BLACKBERRIES

A RATHER elaborate design of hops and blackberries arranged as shown in the illustration on page 13. The sachet is made of white satin jean ; it measures 17 inches wide and 14 inches deep. The flap is 6½ inches deep ; the back and the flap are cut in one piece. Procure a few skeins of Strutt's knitting cotton, No. 6 and No. 8, and 3 yards of torchon lace for trimming. The hops and blackberries, most of the stems, many of the largest leaves, and the buttonhole scollops are worked with the coarsest cotton, and the finest cotton is reserved for small leaves, tendrils, and the minute portions of the design.

Having traced the design upon the material, consider first the working of the front of the pocket ; you will observe a thick, important looking stem, almost in the centre of the pocket ; this is formed by working four lines of crewel stitch very closely and flatly side by side. The other thick stems are embroidered in highly raised

Comb-Bag. Design of Passion Flowers

overcasting, and the slender stems variously in cord stitch, crewel stitch, and snail-trail stitch. The blackberries are simulated in the usual manner by clusters of French knots worked closely together, placing large knots in the centre, and small knots by the outline, to produce the raised spherical appearance of the natural berry. The hops are composed of a number of " loop like " sections of buttonhole stitch. A reference to the engraving will show the shape of the loops, and the manner in which they are grouped together, beginning at the lower end of the hop, and working as it were in " layers " upwards, each succeeding loop of stitches lapping a little way over its predecessor. A large leaf outlined with small French knots, and filled with a veining of crewel stitch and bullion stitches, is familiar to all Mountmellick workers. Above this leaf, and a little to the left thereof, is a very pretty large leaf, or it may be considered as a group of three leaves clustered together, embroidered in a new and novel manner. The margin is outlined in raised satin stitch, the stitches being for the most part long and perfectly

even on the side nearest to the centre of the leaf, but on the outside, where the edge is serrated, the stitches are longer or shorter according to the tracing. The interior of the leaf is filled with bullion stitches or " worms," as they are sometimes called, placed close together side by side obliquely across the leaf ; this is particularly effective. Another large leaf, occupying the space between this leaf and a bunch of hops, is executed in Indian filling, which stitch is explained on page 4 in No. 69, " Weldon's Practical Needlework Series," and need not be again detailed here. Two groups of effective leaves, a little further to the left, are outlined with cable-plait stitch, a line of crewel stitch denotes the mid-rib, and spikes of bullion stitches branch out thence on either side. Two smaller groups of leaves, on the same side of the pocket, are embroidered after the style of leaf 8 on the sampler, page 11, No. 69 ; these are very pretty leaves. Several more pretty leaves will be seen on the right-hand side of the pocket, one half of each leaf is worked in raised satin stitch, extending from the mid-rib to the margin of the leaf, and the other half is " open " being simply outlined with crewel stitch, and rendered effective by means of four or five stem-stitch veinings, proceeding from the raised satin stitch to within a short distance of the outline. When the floral design on the pocket is finished, leave it, and proceed with the flap, which is embroidered to correspond. The buttonhole stitching, round the " turndown " of the flap, is worked in the form of scollops, in stitches of graduated length, the first stitch long, and each successive stitch shorter till six stitches are done, when make another long stitch like the first, and continue. Similar scollops are worked round the pocket, and by taking the stitches through both pieces of material, the pocket may in this way be joined to the back of the sachet. The sachet is then edged with torchon lace, put on full, as shown in the engraving.

BORDER FOR A FIVE-O'CLOCK OR OCCASIONAL TEA-CLOTH.

THIS is a handsome design for a border in raised Mountmellick, and one that need not be too finely executed, as it is intended to be bold in appearance and outline. Procure a square of the best quality white satin jean, or strong holland, a supply of Strutt's No. 8 knitting cotton, and a few yards of very narrow white braid to lay down as a scolloped couching above the vandyked points and also in places in the floral portion of the design. Trace the entire outline of the border upon the material before commencing to work, contriving to bring in the pattern in turning the corners in as skilful a manner as possible. First, lay down the braid in position and couch it with buttonhole stitches placed at regular intervals of space one from the other, as is clearly apparent in the engraving. The greater part of the floral design is worked in thickly raised buttonhole stitch, but the stem and most of the tendrils are carried out in raised satin stitch to afford variety ; in neither of these is the braid used, but threads of cotton are run along the outline to serve for a padding. The flame flowers are entirely outlined with raised buttonholing, excepting the vein that arches across the middle, and this is sparsely worked with buttonhole stitches over braid to correspond with the scollops already done; the lower portion of the flower is studded with round spots of satin stitch or with simple cross-stitches; both workings are shown in the engraving; the flower that has satin-stitch spots in the base has an embroidered star in each of its petals, and the flower that has cross-stitches in the base has large round spots of satin stitch in its petals, while below the arched vein the flowers are similarly decorated with five upright bullion stitches. The star-shaped flowers are defined by the pretty stitch known as cable plait, which is represented in clear detail, Fig. 8, No. 45, "Weldon's Practical Needlework Series;" a circle of raised satin stitch indicates the heart or centre of the flower, and the spaces in the petals are filled with pear-shaped lobes of raised satin stitch, one lobe in each petal. The leaves are treated conventionally, and though of various shapes and sizes are all outlined with highly raised buttonhole stitch, and the filling is tastefully selected according to

The border may be utilised for a tray-cloth or trimming for an apron, and other purposes. The original measures about 5 inches in width. The outer margin of the fabric beyond the vandyked scollops may, if desired, be cut away, after the fashion of English Embroidery.

ANTIQUE BORDER FOR A FIVE-O'CLOCK OR OCCASIONAL TEA-CLOTH.

THE engraving represents an antique scroll arranged for a border; this is worked in the original with No. 10 Strutt's knitting cotton upon white satin jean, and measures in its entirety 6 inches deep, but the two marginal insertions take up 1 inch, so that 5 inches only are occupied with the scroll, which is bold in character, lacy in appearance, and very handsome if correctly worked. When the

D'Oyley. Mountain Ash.

the space at command, thus, some of the leaves are veined with feather stitch, others with a mixture of feather stitch and bullion stitch, others are studded with French knots, or with dot stitch, and some have simply a mid-rib of knot stitches, or of point de reprise and button-stitch loops; indeed, any description of filling may be introduced according to taste, in the leaves as well as in the flowers, provided that uniformity is preserved in the thick outlining which is the characteristic of this design.

The vandyked edge is embroidered after the floral pattern is accomplished; this consists of a kind of a trefoil planted in the centre of each vandyke, or scollop, which trefoil as well as the marginal edge of the other part of each vandyke is worked in close button-holing over a foundation of thickly raised darned threads, the three sections of the trefoil are embroidered with loops of daisy stitch, and a couple of leviathan cross-stitches are employed to fill in the space on each side.

design is traced upon the material in readiness for commencing operations, the first proceeding is to embroider in cable-plait stitch the straight lines that define the relative portions of the pattern; of these there are two on each side the border, forming as it were a boundary to the two narrow insertions; if you do not understand cable-plait stitch, turn to page 5, No. 45, "Weldon's Practical Needlework Series," where it appears illustrated in full working size with all necessary instructions. The narrow insertions are filled in with long stitches taken in diamond fashion across and across the space that intervenes between the two lines of cable plait, and a French knot is worked in the centre of each diamond, and a straight stitch passes over the crossed threads, in the manner shown in the engraving.

Now as regards the **Scroll.** The outline of every leaf, flower, and lobe, is carefully delineated with a laid thread, which may either be a thread of coarse knitting cotton, or a linen thread, or a thread of Japanese cord, held in place by being couched with a stitch taken across it at regular intervals. The petals of the flowers are embroidered, two of them with closely worked Indian filling, and four with the buttonhole-stitch filling known to point lace workers as "Point de Sorrento." Looking at the engraving you will see the buttonhole stitches are placed in parallel lines, two stitches close together, then a little space, and two more stitches; in successive lines the buttonhole stitches are worked over the thread at the top of the space, taking the needle always through the material for the sake of firmness: this is a very pretty and lacy filling if the rows

with small French knots; and another leaf is prettily embroidered with button-stitch loops made exactly in the same way as button-stitch loops are made on dresses. The lobes are filled entirely with a diamond filling of crossed threads held in place with a small straight stitch wherever the threads of the diamonds cross each other. Although close work this border presents no difficulty to a fairly skilful embroiderer, and it will well repay the care and attention bestowed upon it.

As a finish to the extreme edge of the table-cloth a deep hem would be sufficient, or to render the work still more elaborate a

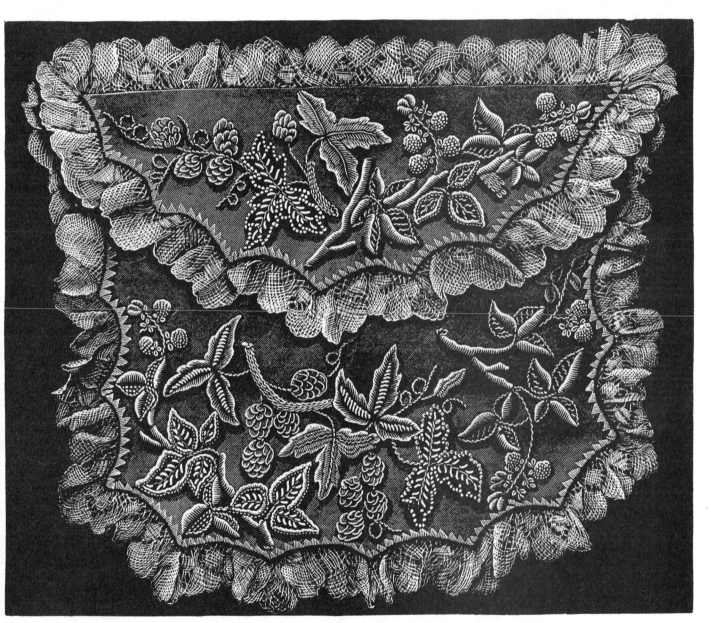

Nightdress Sachet.   Design of Hops and Blackberries.

are kept even and the buttonhole stitches all of equal size. Certain leaves on the outside of the scroll are worked in brick couching, which is accomplished in a very simple manner; long stitches are taken the lengthways of the leaf, and must lie perfectly straight and flat and close together, with smaller stitches in the curves of the leaf, filling the leaf completely with a surface of smooth threads, then other long stitches are taken across the leaf diagonally, not close together, but with a reasonable space between each stitch; these latter stitches are then held in place by dot stitches, or securing stitches, alternating as shown in each successive row. A small leaf, almost in the centre of the design, is completely filled

frill of torchon lace would be effective. In place of the lower bordering, the material could be scolloped and finished with button-hole stitch and torchon lace, after the style shown by the night-dress sachet on this page. Equal, too, is this handsome design to being reproduced on faced cloth, worked with coloured silks, in which case the outlining would be done with fine gold thread, couched down with silk stitches. Two rows of the gold thread stand out well, and the bordering, shown in the illustration, could then be replaced by four or five rows of gold thread put on in a waved design, and cloth goods would be pinked out as a finish to the extreme edge.

Border for a Five-o'Clock or Occasional Tea-Cloth.

Antique Border for a Five-o'Clock or Occasional Tea-Cloth

WELDON'S PRACTICAL
MOUNTMELLICK EMBROIDERY

(SIXTH SERIES.)

New and Original Designs for Leaves and Fillings, Table-Cover, Borders, Comb-Bag, &c.

THIRTY-THREE ILLUSTRATIONS.

MOUNTMELLICK EMBROIDERY.

THE present issue contains a varied assortment of original and valuable designs in Mountmellick Embroidery illustrative of new stitches, conventionally treated borders, table-cover, comb-bag, &c.; and as in the execution of this favourite embroidery it is of the utmost importance that all minor details, such as leaves, stems, and fillings, should receive their due share of attention and not in any way be slurred over, we have had twenty-two examples of leaves worked in the newest and prettiest style, many of them delicately filled with ornamental stitches, which all are engraved in the full actual size, so that every stitch is perceivable, and no manner of doubt can exist as to the possibility of copying and correctly reproducing the same, while to aid the inexperienced and to afford information to those who require to go well into the subject, very explicit instructions for each example are conveyed in the letter-press.

The first principles of Mountmellick Embroidery, and a great number of stitches appertaining to the successful execution of this pleasing work, are fully explained and illustrated in No. 45, "Weldon's Practical Needlework Series." No. 47 contains a variety of sprays, mats, and a most lovely toilet-cover executed in a design of lilies and passion flowers. No. 50 is devoted to further examples, including a coat of arms, a corner for a quilt, a pincushion, comb-bags, &c. No. 69 has, among other things, a sampler of twenty handsomely worked leaves, an exquisite tray-cloth finely embroidered in pomegranates, and a toilet-cover in blackberries. No. 79 comprises two pretty d'oyleys, nightdress sachets and comb-bags, a pillow-sham, and a good assortment of borders and corners. These five numbers, together with the issue now brought forward, should be in the possession of every embroiderer; they contain upwards of 180 engravings, and form the most complete and useful treatise published on Mountmellick Embroidery.

GORDON KNOT STITCH.

THIS new stitch bears a resemblance to the well-known "snail-trail stitch," Fig. 5, No. 45, "Weldon's Practical Needlework Series," and like it is used for fine stems, outlines, and light tracery, but the knot is more distinct than the snail-trail stitch knot. It may be worked with the material held straight towards you, or from right to left; we will explain the former manner as exemplified in the engraving, and when you understand the stitch you will see how to manage it in the other direction. Bring up the needle and cotton to the front of the fabric in the place where you desire to commence working, hold the cotton for an instant under the left-hand thumb, pass the needle from right to left under the cotton so held, and with a gentle movement of the thumb push the cotton upwards under the point of the needle; turn all the cotton upwards, reverse the position of the needle from left to right, and insert it horizontally to take up a thread or two of the material in the place where the knot is to be formed, that is, at the distance of one-eighth of an inch or so below where the cotton was brought out; turn the cotton downwards under the point of the needle (the position now is as shown in the engraving), and draw carefully through. You will have a long stitch and a knot stitch. All succeeding knots are formed in the same way, and all equidistant one from the other. The stitch requires practice, but is done quickly enough when once you get into the way of it.

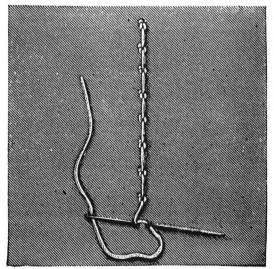

Gordon Knot Stitch.

THORN STITCH.

THORN STITCH is a combination of coral stitch and French knots, and is pretty for stems of medium width, and also for the outlining of leaves and petals. Begin by tracing two parallel lines to denote the width the thorn stitch is required to be. Bring the needle and cotton out at the top midway between the two lines, hold the cotton

4

under the left-hand thumb, insert the needle to take up five or six threads of material straight on the line to the left-hand side, and pass the point of the needle over the cotton held by the thumb and draw through; place the thumb again upon the cotton and make a similar stitch on the line on the right-hand side and draw through; both the stitches are set in perpendicularly, but the second stitch must be slightly lower than the first; a strand of cotton on the surface of the material connects the two stitches together, and so far the work is precisely identical with "Single Coral Stitch," Fig. 10, No. 45, "Weldon's Practical Needlework Series." But now comes the difference which effects such an improvement and transforms an otherwise simple stitch into a particularly ornamental one: Retain-

Fig. 1.—LEAF WITH ORNAMENTAL FILLING.

THE outline of this leaf is executed in crewel stitch; the filling is commenced by inserting the needle first on the right and then on the left-hand side of the leaf, taking up each time a small piece of material below the crewel stitch outline; these stitches themselves are invisible, as they appear only on the wrong side of the material, but from each stitch a strand of cotton is carried across the surface of the leaf, and if the stitches are all the same size these strands of cotton will lie at regular intervals one from another, vertically, across the leaf, as shown in the engraving. The leaf is then further embellished by working a line of cross-stitches straight down its centre, doing one cross-stitch in the middle of each of the spaces between

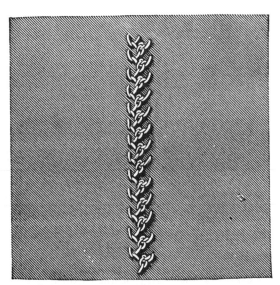

Thorn Stitch.

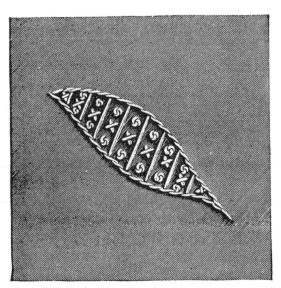

Fig. 1.—Leaf with Ornamental Filling.

Fig. 2.—A Broad Palmate Leaf deeply serrated.

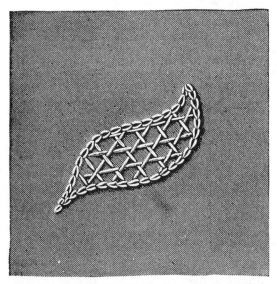

Fig. 3.—A Leaf filled with Brussels Net Stitch.

ing the cotton again under the left-hand thumb, pass the point of the needle under the cotton, and over and under, and over and under the cotton again, keep the twist close on the needle and the cotton still under pressure of thumb and turn the point of the needle upwards and carry it over the strand that runs across from the first to the second stitch, and inserting it in the material, bring it out below the strand and midway between the lines and over the cotton held by the thumb, and draw through, being careful not to disarrange the twist, which when drawn up closely forms a knot. Continue working by the above instruction, and you will produce a stem of thorn stitch as represented in the engraving.

the strands; then a French knot on each side of each cross-stitch will tastefully occupy what little space there still remains between the cross-stitches and the outline, and so the leaf will be completed.

Fig. 2.—A PROAD PALMATE LEAF DEEPLY SERRATED.

HERE is a handsome bold leaf suitable for a large piece of work. The centre vein or mid-rib is first to be embroidered in closely set feather stitch, called by the ancients "opus plumarium," from the resemblance which its long stitches, radiating alike to right and left, bear to the feathers of a bird; it commences with a narrow peak at the top, and gradually widens to nearly three-eighths of an inch, at which width it is kept till a sufficient length (nearly two inches) brings you to the bottom. The serrated edges of the leaf are worked in buttonhole stitch with a little open space between the teeth of each stitch, work first the angular piece at the top of the leaf immediately above the plume, turn the plume sideways and do a series of little detached curved streaks of buttonhole stitch on the right side of the leaf, not too near the plume, but at the distance shown in the engraving, carry the last curved streak (which ends at the base of the plume) further on to the left of the leaf in corresponding shape to that done on the left side, turning the material in the hand

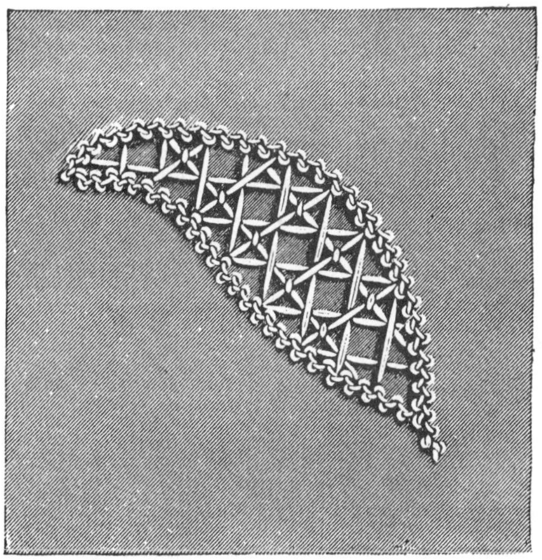

stitches from one side of the leaf to the other side in an oblique direction; across these work other long stitches slanting in the contrary direction; and so arranged that the two sets of stitches form a series of meshes of open diamond net work; then three long stitches are to be run the parallel way of the leaf, in darning fashion, passing the needle alternately over and under the net-like threads of the open diamonds, and the leaf will appear as perfect as in the engraving.

Fig. 4.—LEAF FILLED WITH DOUBLE BRUSSELS NET STITCH.

THIS leaf shows a bold outline executed in the pretty cable

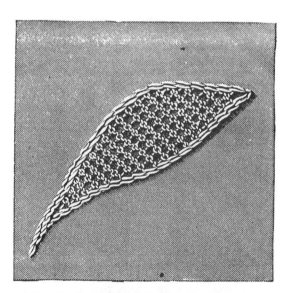

Fig. 4.—Leaf filled with Double Brussels Net Stitch.

Fig. 5.—Leaf filled with Pyramid Stitch.

Fig. 6.—Leaf filled with Point de Sorrento.

Fig. 7.—Leaf edged with Indented Overcasting.

so as to hold it with convenience, and continue working this side to correspond with the side that is already done. There should be space enough between the curved streaks of buttonhole stitch and the plume to contain two rows of medium-sized French knots.

Fig. 3.—A LEAF FILLED WITH BRUSSELS NET STITCH.

THIS is a pretty leaf, very light and lacy in appearance, the outline being simple chain stitch and the interior open work in imitation of Brussels net. This latter is produced by carrying long

plait stitch, for explanation of which see Fig. 8, No. 45, "Weldon's Practical Needlework Series;" also the net work is slightly more complicated than in the previous description, for, after the cable plait outline is accomplished, you will work across and across the narrow way of the leaf, taking a stitch first on the right-hand side and then on the left close against the outline, and in such a manner that though the stitches themselves—being taken through the material—do not show, a strand of cotton from stitch to stitch is carried quite across the inner surface of the leaf at intervals of about one-eighth of an inch apart; then you must arrange the two oblique lines of threads as instructed in the previous example; and finish by darning two stitches the long way of the leaf through the network of threads in such a manner as to cross the first set of threads in the exact centre of two lines of diamonds, and secure these in position by working the first half of a cross-stitch thereupon as represented in the illustration.

Fig. 5.—LEAF FILLED WITH PYRAMID STITCH.

HERE is shown a particularly elegant leaf in a new style of working. The outline is designed in crewel stitch, and the interior is entirely filled with the stitch known familiarly to lace workers by

Fig. 6.—LEAF WORKED IN POINT DE SORRENTO

THE outline of this leaf is embroidered in chain stitch, while the centre is completely occupied with a network of buttonhole stitches worked in pairs—the same stitch which by lace workers is technically termed "Point de Sorrento." This is executed in rows backwards and forwards—in the first row you work the buttonhole stitches into the material, putting two stitches closely together, then leaving a little space, and doing two more stitches, and so on; but in the following rows, after beginning by steadying the turn of the row into the material close against the outline, you will form each pair

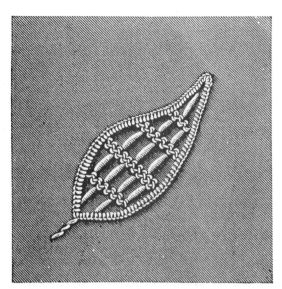

Fig. 8.—Leaf: Ornamented with Bullion Stitch and Bars of Cable Plait.

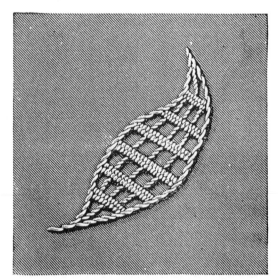

Fig. 9.—Leaf: Twisted Threads and Point de Reprise.

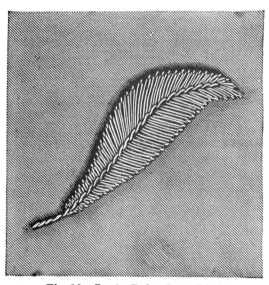

Fig. 10.—Leaf: Daisy Loop Stitch.

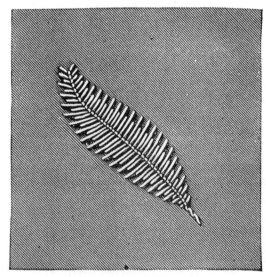

Fig. 11.—Leaf: Spike Stitch.

the name of "pyramid stitch," which adapts itself well to Mountmellick Embroidery, and is really nothing more than a series of little triangles worked in overcast or smooth satin stitch. Begin near the base of the leaf, and take the first satin stitch straight across the leaf for the purpose of forming the bottom of the first pyramid, then each successive stitch above this is to be a trifle shorter and shorter, until, in from six to eight stitches, the top is reached, where a very tiny stitch, no larger than a dot stitch, is required to complete the pyramid or triangle. As depicted in the engraving, there are triangular-shaped spaces of material visible between the worked pyramids, and the two alternate together in a very pleasing manner.

of buttonhole stitches upon the thread that extends along the space between the buttonhole stitches of the preceding row, and thus the pairs of buttonhole stitches in every row alternate with each other, and a pretty dice-patterned network is produced as shown in the engraving.

Fig. 7.—LEAF EDGED WITH INDENTED OVERCASTING.

A NARROW leaf, elegant in itself, and useful to intermix with leaves of a larger and heavier character. Trace as usual, and delineate the mid vein by a single thread of cotton held down at intervals by a couch-stitch. Pad thickly the margin that is to be covered with overcasting, and then proceed in stitches of alternate lengths—the first stitch must embrace the padding and hold it compactly in the position it is required to lie, the second stitch is level with the first in the interior of the leaf, but projects considerably further outside beyond the padding—and these two stitches are repeated, and the result is decidedly natty and pleasing.

Fig. 8.—LEAF ORNAMENTED WITH BULLION STITCH AND BARS OF CABLE PLAIT

THE contour of this leaf is first of all to be delineated by a series of small close buttonhole stitches. Then four bars of cable plait are

again repeated. The leaf is handsome when nicely worked, and a clever embroiderer will not experience difficulty in managing it.

Fig. 9.—LEAF: TWISTED THREADS AND POINT DE REPRISE.

HERE we see a leaf embroidered in quite a novel style, and very light and tasteful it is when correctly rendered. The outline is sufficiently simple, being carried out in crewel stitch, which though so easy of execution is generally liked because it produces an excellent result with only a small amount of labour. After the

Fig. 12.—Long Narrow Leaf in Buttonhole Stitch and Spike Stitch.

Fig. 13.—Leaf with Saw Tooth Outline.

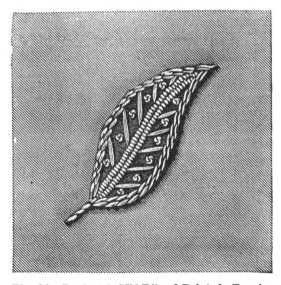

Fig. 14.—Leaf with Mid-Rib of Point de Reprise.

Fig. 15.—Leaf: Overcast and Spike Stitch.

to be embroidered horizontally across the leaf, as represented in the engraving, and between these bars are ornamental bullion stitches, otherwise termed worm stitches, extending horizontally from bar to bar; thus, one bullion stitch reaches from the topmost bar to nearly the tip of the leaf, in the next space two bullion stitches find accommodation, in the next space three stitches, in the next four stitches, while in the lower space at the base of the leaf there is room for two stitches only. The correct method of working bullion stitches has been already detailed, see Fig. 29, No. 45, and page 14, No. 69, "Weldon's Practical Needlework Series," and need not be

outline is accomplished the next proceeding is to work the six bars of "Point de Reprise" that traverse the inner surface of the leaf; point de reprise is familiar to workers of point lace, and is also used a good deal in drawn thread embroidery, but in case any of our readers may be ignorant of the procedure we will here explain the method of working: Commence by forming four long stitches, close together and smooth and even one with another, like long satin stitches, right across from side to side of the leaf; these long stitches have no occasion to appear at all on the back of the material, for by taking up a few threads of the material close against and level with the outline they may stretch from side to side on the surface only. Now having the needle and cotton on the right side of the work, take the needle over the first two of the long threads and under the second two, and draw through, turn the needle the reverse way and pass it over the two threads it just went under, and under the two threads it before went over, and draw through, and continue this in-and-out darning until the bar is well covered with stitches, never taking the needle through the material but only over and under the threads; and proceed in the same manner with the other bars successively. Next consider the twisted stitches, of which the middle one is first to be formulated—Bring the needle and cotton up to the front of the material close to the point of the leaf, take a small running stitch in the material in the centre of the leaf below the first bar of point de reprise, a similar stitch under the second bar, and so on, till you arrive at the base; here pass the needle and cotton to the back of the material and bring it up again to the front within a thread or two of the same place. You will now see a single line or strand of cotton running as it were the whole way down the centre of the leaf from the tip to the base, hidden only by the bars of point de reprise which apparently bridge over it; pass the needle and cotton four times under and over the first portion of the strand and you will get a twisted stitch, pass the needle and cotton under the bar and three or four times under and over the next portion of the strand, and continue the twisted stitch in the same way up to point of the leaf. Make two more twisted stitches, one on each side of the preceding, but reaching in length merely from the first to the last bar of point de reprise. The leaf will now appear as represented in the engraving.

Fig. 10.—LEAF IN DAISY LOOP STITCH.

THIS is a graceful leaf if smoothly worked, and moreover is quite easy to manipulate. Nearly every one is acquainted with daisy loop stitch. The leaf is traced in the usual manner. Hold the tracing in such a position as to work from left to right, and beginning by the base of the leaf, bring up the needle and cotton to the front upon the mid-rib line, and draw through, then with the cotton held under the left-hand thumb as if about to do buttonholing, insert the needle in the same place from whence it has just been drawn through, and bring it forward upon the outline, passing over the cotton held by the thumb, and draw through, and you have a loop similar to a chain-stitch loop; insert the needle outside this loop to the back of the material and bring it out upon the mid-rib in readiness for another daisy stitch, and draw through, so forming a tiny straight stitch over the tip of the daisy loop stitch, which besides being ornamental serves to hold the loop in place. Every successive daisy loop stitch is worked in the same way, they are placed closely together, and they lengthen considerably in accordance with the contour of the leaf, as you will perceive by consulting the illustration. After the daisy loop stitch is complete the leaf is finished by working a mid-rib of crewel stitch, and the same is continued as a stem.

Fig. 11.—LEAF WORKED IN SPIKE STITCH.

AN extremely simple leaf, but one that looks well mingled with others that are larger and more elaborate. It may be commenced at the tip or at the base, as preferred. Bring the needle and cotton up to the front of the material on the outline nearest to you; insert it in the opposite outline and bring it up a little distance *within* the outline from whence you started, and draw through, insert the needle a little distance *within* the opposite outline, and bring it up on the outline nearest to you; and go on in this way, alternately a long stitch and a short stitch, not quite closely together, and yet not much perceptible space apart. You will find all the stitches must get considerably longer in the centre of the leaf than at either end; the actual length is entirely guided by the tracing, but all the long stitches must be level with one another, and the short stitches also level with themselves, and this it is that gives the jagged edge to the leaf as shown in the engraving. A line of neat back-stitching is carried down the centre of the leaf, one back-stitch to each spike stitch, and this, while forming a mid-rib, serves also to steady the spike stitches, and adds considerably to the appearance of the leaf.

Fig. 12.—LONG NARROW LEAF IN BUTTON-HOLE STITCH AND SPIKE STITCH.

THE principal portion of this leaf consists of two rows of close evenly set buttonhole stitches, placed together in opposite position; that is, with the teeth of the stitches upon the mid-rib, and conse-

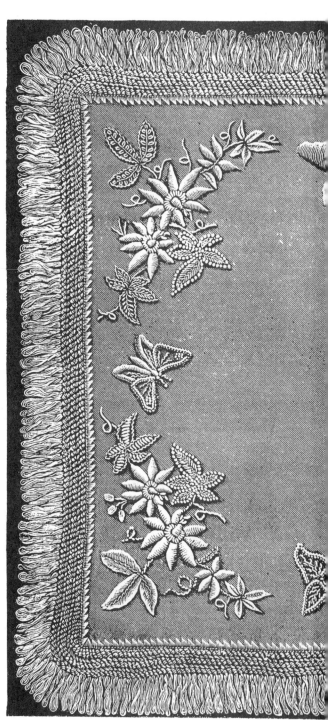

Sn

quently the loops of the stitches come upon the outline of the leaf. The severity of this outline is relieved by an edging of spike stitches, and down the mid-rib where the buttonhole stitches meet, you will do a line of back-stitching consisting of one short stitch and one long stitch alternately, as is evident in the engraving.

Fig. 13.—LEAF WITH SAW-TOOTH OUTLINE.

The outline of this pretty leaf is produced by working alternately two tall and two short buttonhole stitches, in the style which technically is called "saw-tooth buttonholing" (see Fig. 22, No. 45, "Weldon's Practical Needlework Series"); the indentations made

Table-Cover.

by the teeth of the stitches are arranged to point towards the interior of the leaf that is the subject of the present example, and therefore the smooth, even loops of the stitches constitute the margin. The centre of the leaf is decorated with a sprig of open feather stitch.

Fig. 14.—LEAF WITH MID-RIB OF POINT DE REPRISE.

Here again is a novel arrangement of stitches which combine together in forming an exceedingly effective leaf. The outline is first of all embroidered in chain stitch; then attention must be paid to the mid-rib executed in point de reprise, and for this you must first of all lay four strands of cotton upon the surface of the material reaching from the tip to the bottom of the leaf like the strings of a violin, taking the needle to the back only at these points so as to avoid making corresponding long threads on the wrong side of the fabric. When the four strands are in order, and the needle and cotton on the right side of the work, pass the needle over the first two threads and under the second two threads and draw through, reverse the position of the needle and pass it over the two threads it just went under and under the two threads it before went over and draw through, and continue darning in this manner along the whole length of the mid-rib. Next arrange four or five spike stitches at regular intervals on each side of the mid-rib, slanting upwards therefrom to the outline; and finally decorate the leaf with French knots, making one knot in the centre of each space between the spike stitches.

Fig. 15.—LEAF: OVERCAST AND SPIKE STITCH.

The outline of this pretty open leaf is defined in raised overcasting, that is to say, a narrow margin of space within the tracing is filled with threads darned tolerably thickly on the surface of the material, and these threads are afterwards overcast, or sewn smoothly over, the stitches now taking a vertical direction, as will be seen by consulting the illustration. The outer margin is surrounded with spike stitches. The centre is occupied by a feather-stitch veining.

Fig. 16.—LEAF, CLOSELY WORKED IN BACK STITCH AND FRENCH KNOTS.

A novel leaf, worked in back-stitching and French knots, with its margin of cross-stitch, and is a particularly handsome design, very suitable for introducing into large pieces of work. The outline is drawn in the usual manner, and at present serves merely as a guide to indicate how far the back-stitching may extend. Commence stitching at the tip of the leaf and proceed in a slanting direction towards the left-hand side, taking up always four threads at a time—i.e., two threads backwards and two threads forwards, as in plain needlework; turn when you reach the outline on the side of the leaf and start another row of stitches to run parallel with the row you have just done and at the distance of about six threads therefrom, and continue across and across from the outline on one side the leaf to the outline on the opposite side, always in the same vertical direction, and always leaving the same amount of space between the rows, till the surface of the leaf is fairly well covered with stitching; then proceed with more stitching in cross-bar fashion, making a perfect diamond network of stitches. A line of French knots is to be embroidered upon the diamond network up the centre of the leaf, also a few French knots on each side, as represented in the engraving. Edge the margin of the leaf with cross stitches.

Fig. 17.—LEAF WITH SCOLLOPED OUTLINE.

An effective style of leaf is shown here, and one that is likely to be a favourite. In shape it is long and slender; the outline consists of smooth, flat buttonholing scolloped on the outside margin of the leaf, or if liked, the buttonholing may be raised by padding; a row of cable-plait is carried up the centre of the leaf to simulate a mid-rib.

Fig. 18.—A LIGHT PRETTY LEAF.

TRACE the outline in the usual way, and work it partly in feather stitch and partly in crewel stitch, as depicted in the engraving. Embroider a row of medium-sized French knots up the middle of the interior, and a surrounding of French knots upon the outside margin, and this pretty leaf will be finished.

Fig. 19.—LEAF WITH CABLE-PLAIT VEINING.

THIS is a good-sized, bold patterned leaf, of open character, especially suitable for large pieces of work where quick execution is

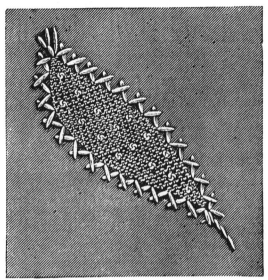

Fig. 16.--Leaf, closely worked in Back-stitch and French Knots.

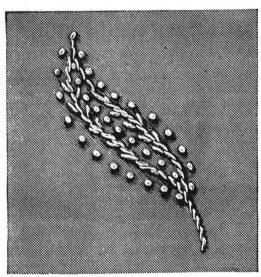

Fig. 18.—A Light Pretty Leaf.

desired. It is simply outlined with crewel stitch; the mid-rib also is of crewel stitch except at the top, where it changes into cable-plait to harmonise with the veins, which branch out from the mid-rib to the outline on each side of the leaf; in all these veins it is a good plan to make the cable-plait quite narrow against the mid-rib and gradually increase the width as it approaches the outline.

Fig. 20.—LEAF: SATIN STITCH AND BACK-STITCH.

A CHARMING leaf is formulated in close embroidery, employing crewel stitch, satin stitch, back-stitch, and couching. Begin with

the outline, which is to be couched with a strand of cotton two sizes coarser than the cotton you are using for the embroidery. Next, work in crewel stitch the mid-rib up the centre of the leaf. After this, turn your attention to the three V-shaped bars, and arrange for them to appear upon the leaf as shown in the engraving, tracing two lines for each bar, as a guide whereby the satin stitch may be confined within the required limit; the satin stitches are taken in a

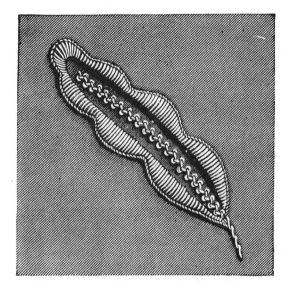

Fig. 17.—Leaf with Scolloped Outline.

Fig. 19.—Leaf with Cable-Plait Veining.

straight direction within the two lines, close together, and perfectly even one with another. The space between the bars, and also the space at the top and bottom of the leaf, is now to be closely filled with rows of neat back-stitching, slanting in the same direction as the bars slant, the stitches close and small, and the rows in even line and regular, at very little distance one from the other; this takes some time to accomplish, but the effect is very good when finished.

Fig. 21.—LEAF WITH COUCHED OUTLINE.

THE outline of this leaf is couched with a piece of piping cord, which when laid carefully upon the tracing is held in position by neat stitches passing over it at regularly spaced intervals, as will be understood by referring to the engraving, and a particularly bold and firm outline is in this manner formed; but four or five strands of cotton laid closely together will answer the purpose almost equally well if a piping cord is not at hand. Trace the situation the V-shaped veinings are to occupy; but before working these, arrange six lines of cotton to run lengthways perpendicularly up the leaf, three lines on each side of the mid-rib, in position as shown in the engraving; by taking short stitches into the material below the V-shaped veinings these lines of cotton will be steadied to the contour of the leaf; they are now to be converted into twisted threads by passing the needle and cotton round each in such a manner as to "twist" the second thread over the first. The working of these twisted threads and also the method of producing the V-shaped veinings, which are worked in point de reprise, will be readily comprehended by turning to Fig. 9, where both stitches are minutely described. The leaf will be completed by embroidering a mid-rib of crewel stitch.

Fig 22.—LEAF WORKED IN RAISED PICOTS.

THE raised picots of which this leaf is composed are worked some-

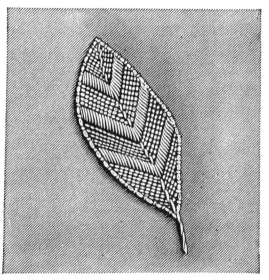

Fig. 20.—Leaf: Satin Stitch and Back Stitch.

the same place from whence it came, and pass the needle under the cotton held by the thumb, and draw through, being careful not to disarrange the twist that now is on the top of the needle; pass the needle below the picot just formed, to the back of the work, and bring it up just within the outline on the right-hand side a little lower down the leaf, and make another picot stitch as described above; and when this is done pass the needle to the back below the picot and bring it up in the picot again, make a short running stitch upon the surface of the material, and take about two threads of material on the needle, and you now will be in position for working a picot close to the outline on the left-hand side of the leaf to correspond with the picot on the right-hand side; the running stitch extends across the leaf between these two picots, and this is the first row. Take the needle and cotton across the back of the fabric to the left-hand side of the leaf in readiness to work the second row, make the first picot and the first running stitch as instructed above; the second picot will require to be formed in the centre of the leaf and must be made upon the running stitch of the previous row, taking the needle also through the fabric as before, finish this picot with a running stitch, and make a third picot by the outline on the left-hand side of the leaf, and thus three picots and two running stitches will be comprised in the second row. Proceed with every succeeding row in the same manner from right to left, increasing one picot and one running stitch in every row as the leaf widens, and

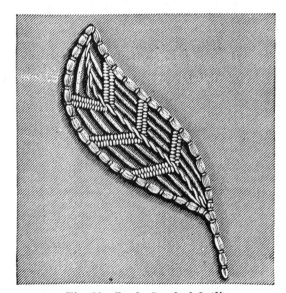

Fig. 21.—Leaf: Couched Outline.

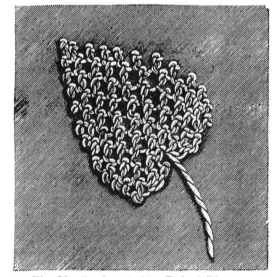

Fig. 22.—Leaf worked in Raised Picots.

thing after the manner of French knots, but a small running stitch is employed to connect the picots one with another, and this entirely alters the character of the embroidery, and converts what would otherwise be an ordinary knot stitch into a stitch having the appearance of picots standing raised upon a network ground. Trace the outline as usual, and begin working at the top of the leaf; bring up the needle and cotton a few threads below the tip of the leaf, hold the cotton under the left-hand thumb and pass the point of the needle three times under and over the cotton, and then, still retaining the cotton under the thumb, lift the point of the needle upwards and insert it in the outline just at the tip of the leaf and bring it out in

contract the stitches at the base; finish with a short crewel-stitched stem, and the leaf will appear as represented in the engraving.

SMALL TABLE-COVER.

A USEFUL cover for a small table can be worked in Mountmellick embroidery in a design of passion flowers, clematis, and butterflies, as represented in the accompanying engraving. The original cover measures 26 inches by 24 inches; white satin jean is employed for the foundation and the work is executed in bold style with Strutt's

12

No. 6 best knitting cotton. Each corner of the cloth is occupied with a spray consisting of two passion flowers, several leaves, and tendrils; a small branch of clematis is placed in the centre of each of the two longest sides, and a butterfly in the centre of each of the two other sides. Enlarge the design to the requisite size, and trace it upon the satin jean in the usual manner. Then, if you will turn to page 12, No. 47, "Weldon's Practical Needlework Series," you will see two PASSION FLOWERS and two leaves illustrated so clearly that every stitch can be readily copied; working instructions are supplied with the example, and the same will suffice to go by in the present instance, remembering to reproduce the leaves as nearly as possible

Turret Buttonholing.

HOW TO MITRE THE CORNERS.

in the stitches in which they here appear. The CLEMATIS FLOWER has four petals embroidered entirely in Indian filling; the centre consists of a circular boss of satin stitch, from which four worm stitches jut forward at regular intervals; the stem is of crewel stitch; the leaves are prettily outlined with cable plait and filled with a mid-rib and veining of crewel stitch. The BUTTERFLIES are effective looking, the head and body is well padded and covered as represented in the engraving with highly raised overcasting; two tiny French knots simulate eyes, and the antennæ are depicted in crewel stitch tipped by a French knot; the two back wings are outlined with deeply set buttonhole stitches, and veins of crewel stitch are employed as a filling; the two front wings are margined with the pretty stitch known as cable plait, a little veining is arranged upon the sides nearest the body, and a circular group of French knots will nicely imitate the spot of colour in the furthest corner, and thus a butterfly will be finished.

The table cover is embroidered all round with an edging of buttonholing, the stitches go in sixes, the first stitch very small, the next a trifle higher, and so on, till the sixth stitch is the highest of all; this looks exceedingly well when a good piece is accomplished; it must, however, be contrived with the greatest regularity. Then the cloth is bordered with a handsome knitted fringe, using cotton from three different balls, and a pair of No. 10 steel knitting needles. Cast on 12 stitches. Every row is worked alike—make 1 by passing all three strands of cotton round the needle, knit 2 together, knit 1, and repeat this three times. Some people like to *purl* the stitches instead of knitting them. When a sufficient length is accomplished, cast off 7 stitches, break off the cottons and draw the ends through. Unravel the remaining 5 stitches. Sew the fringe by the loops at the top of the heading to the loops of the buttonhole stitching.

TURRET BUTTONHOLING.

HOW TO MITRE THE CORNERS.

THE turret style of buttonholing must be executed with the greatest accuracy—that is to say, both sides of the stitches must fall in a perfectly straight line, and all the corners must be mitred so as to pair with each other, or it will not look well. It is a good plan to make a kind of stencil plate of cardboard and use this as a guide wherewith to trace upon the material the *outside* of the buttonhole-stitching—i.e., the side upon which the loops of the stitches are to come. The lower edge of the cardboard will, of course, be straight to begin with, and from it you must cut pieces out at regular intervals; to manage this draw a series of perpendicular lines standing two and a half inches high from the edge, the first line to be two and a quarter inches from the side, the next line one and a half inches from that, and repeat the lines with these alternate spacings as far as the width of the cardboard will permit. Now draw a short line across the top of all the narrowest spaces at the distance of two and a half inches above the edge of the cardboard; these narrow spaces are all to be cut out, and so you get the shape of the turrets. Place the cardboard in correct position upon the material and outline the turrets for the *loop side* of the buttonhole stitches, moving it forward as required; and three-eighths of an inch above this draw another outline ..hereby the *teeth* of the buttonhole stitches may be kept level; also draw a short slanting line from point to point across the angles of the corners to denote

A Flower Conventionally Treated.

the direction the stitches are to take in mitring the corners. The buttonhole stitch is worked in the usual manner, making the stitches level with the outlines—that is, three-eighths of an inch deep everywhere, excepting at the corners, where each successive stitch gets shorter and shorter in accordance with the slanting line till the extreme point of the corner is reached, when they gradually lengthen in the proportion as they before shortened, the teeth of the stitches meeting in angular fashion, as is most clearly shown in the engraving. When all the buttonhole stitching is accomplished the material is cut away by the edge of the loops of the stitches, and you find

[72]

flaps of solid material alternating with cut-out spaces. Turret buttonholing is generally trimmed with wide torchon lace, which is pleated full upon the back of the buttonhole stitching at the top of an open turret space, and carried on thence straight behind the material to the top of the next turret space where more pleating is set in; this has a very pretty appearance—the lace should be sufficiently wide to hang nicely below the edge of the flaps.

A FLOWER CONVENTIONALLY TREATED.

THIS splendid flower is engraved in the full actual size in which it is worked, and, as will at once be seen, it consists entirely of close, firm embroidery, which renders it very rich and important looking, especially when surrounded with leaves of a light and open character. Procure a piece of satin jean and a little of Strutt's No. 10 and No. 6 knitting cotton; the coarser cotton is only used for the two very long stamens and for padding, the finest is employed for all the other part of the work. Trace the flower exactly to the size and shape represented in the engraving, drawing a short straight line down the centre of each of the eight petals, a circle to denote the circumference to which the corona may extend, and a dot to

must be a *long* one) in the centre of the flower and bring up the point in the same place as previously, and retain it in this position while you wind the cotton round and round the point of the needle as many as thirty or forty times, then holding the twist firmly on the needle draw the needle through and pull the twist upwards to the centre of the flower without in any way disarranging it, and you will have one stamen; the other is made similarly; and each stamen is embraced near its tip by a small bullion stitch passing horizontally across it in the manner shown in engraving. The stem belonging to this flower is outlined with a double row of cable plait, and intermediately dotted with French knots.

BORDER OF FLOWERS CONVENTIONALLY TREATED.

OUR engraving shows a design of flowers conventionally treated, adapted for a five-inch wide border, and embroidered in a bold effective style in a combination of the many pretty stitches used in this favourite department of art needlework. The border is suitable for curtains, for the ends of sideboard-slips and tea-slips, and other purposes. It is executed with No. 10 and No. 6 Strutt's knitting

Border of Flowers Conventionally Treated.

mark the exact centre. Commence work by padding the interior of the corona, which is done by darning round and round in a circle, making the stitches lie as much as possible on the front of the material and on one another till you consider it to be raised sufficiently. Pad each of the petals separately in horseshoe shape, not placing any darning on the straight line that is marked down the centre of the petal, but keeping it all on the space intervening between this and the outline. When the padding is all accomplished, the next proceeding will be the embroidering of the petals, and as you will observe, these are executed in wide buttonhole stitch, taking the stitch always from the little straight line in the centre to the outline, and so covering the padding with a close smooth layer of stitches. The corona consists of a ring or circle of bullion loops, sometimes called "worms;" a great number of these spring from the dot in the centre of the flower, and are carried to the traced line that delineates the circumference of the corona, but other and shorter bullion stitches have to be wedged in between, in the manner which you will at once understand by consulting the illustration, and so a perfect ray of bullion stitches will extend over the padding in the centre of the flower, and thus the corona will be brought to completion. There now only remain the stamens, for which use the coarser cotton, bring the needle and cotton up in the place where the tip of the stamen is designed to rest, insert the needle (which

cotton; No. 10 is used for the chief part of the work, No. 6 for padding and for the stamens of the flowers. Both FLOWERS are in highly raised embroidery; we have had the most solid looking of the two flowers engraved separately in its actual working size in order to show as clearly as possible the manner in which the original flower is so cleverly rendered; full instructions accompany the engraving. The other flower is exactly the same shape and size, the corona and stamens are worked in the same way, but the petals are more open and lacy; these petals are padded close against the outline, which then is defined with a not too wide buttonhole stitching, consequently there remains an open space in the interior of each petal, and this is decorated with a diamond trellis of crossed threads held in place by a simple cross-stitch worked over the threads wherever these cross each other; the effect is decidedly uncommon and pleasing. The BLOSSOMS are outlined with chain stitch, defining as it were eight scolloped sections; a French knot occupies the centre of the blossom, and four pairs of bullion stitches rising herefrom are spread across the surface of the blossom in the manner shown in the engraving; a few French knots are then powdered in the intervening space. The STEM is wide throughout and is outlined on both sides with small neat cable plait, and tiny French knots are dotted at intervals up the centre. Most of the LEAVES will be recognised by experienced Mountmellick workers; in shape they are long and slender; a leaf at the top right-hand side is embroidered one-half in French knots and the other half in indented satin stitch; below this a little to the left is a leaf outlined with small neat buttonhole stitching and a mid-rib of cable plait. A small leaf lower down has an outline of indented satin stitch set round a mid-rib of French knots; another leaf has one section embroidered in raised overcasting and the other section simply margined with crewel stitch, within which is a dotted line of French knots; a leaf a little further to the left looks well with an outline of crewel stitch, a herringbone filling, and an outside border of French knots. A leaf close to the large solid flower is traced down one side with chain-stitch, within this a row of good-sized French knots, then a mid-rib worked in crewel stitch, from which to the right extend a series of daisy loop stitches; a leaf below this has one half embroidered in solid raised overcasting, and the other half—after being outlined with crewel stitch, has the interior filled with crossed threads and dot stitches; a leaf further to the left is on one side

embroidery and knitted fringe. The bag is composed of two pieces of material, 13 inches long by 9 inches deep. The flap is angular shaped, and measures 7 inches across the top and 8 inches in length. Enlarge the design to the shape shown in the engraving, and trace it upon the material for the front and flap of the bag; there is of course no embroidery underneath the flap. The spray upon the flap has a stem worked in snail-trail stitch; the berries are about the size of a pea, each one is padded very thickly with stitches, then the padding is solidified and covered by passing back stitches through and through, so holding the padding firmly in place and at same time covering the surface with a number of tiny dot stitches. A large leaf near the bottom of the flap possesses a mid-rib of feather stitch, and the outline of the leaf, which is deeply serrated, is thickly embellished with French knots. A sprig, standing a little to the right, has six leaves composed of bullion stitches worked in pairs, springing from a slender stem of crewel stitch. A sprig of five leaves on the top left-hand side of the flap is executed through-

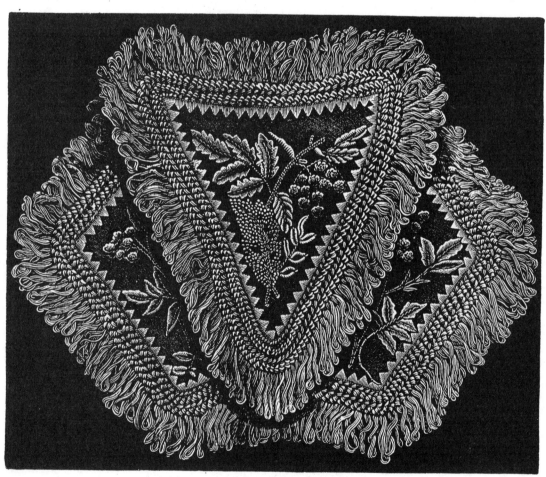

Comb-Bag: Butterfly Shape.

outlined with crewel stitches and spike stitches, and on the other side with cord stitch, while the centre is decorated with six balls of raised satin stitch; and above this we see a leaf outlined with cable plait and filled with a feather-stitch veining, also a leaf embroidered entirely in close, compact feather stitching. The design is repeated for the length required.

COMB-BAG. BUTTERFLY SHAPE.

HERE is a very elegant comb-bag of novel shape, which, being perfectly flat, will conveniently lie upon a dressing table. The design is of mountain ash leaves and berries, a very favourite subject for Mountmellick embroidery, and one that always looks effective and pleasing. Procure half a yard of the best white satin jean and half a pound of Strutt's No. 10 Knitting Cotton for the

out in Indian filling, with a mid-rib of crewel stitch passing up each leaf. One or two ears of wheat are executed in raised overcasting. The front of the bag is embroidered as shown in the engraving. To **make** the **Bag**—Place the front and back together, and work indented buttonhole stitch through both until the pieces are joined upon five of the six sides. Along the sixth side, which is the top of the bag, where the opening is, hem the front of the material, and place the flap in position upon the back and buttonhole-stitch these two together, carrying the buttonhole stitches down the other two sides of the flap; thus the front will open under the top of the flap to receive a brush and comb. One piece of knitted fringe is required to go round the bag, and another piece is carried round the flap. Plenty of fulness must be put at the corners. Instructions for knitting fringe will be found by turning to Fig. 49, No. 45, "Weldon's Practical Needlework Series," and page 6, No. 69, "Weldon's Practical Needlework Series."

WELDON'S PRACTICAL
MOUNTMELLICK EMBROIDERY

(SEVENTH SERIES.)

New and Original Designs for Filling in Leaves, Toilet Mats, Pillow Shams, Brush and Comb Sachet, Tray Cloth, &c.

THIRTEEN ILLUSTRATIONS.

A FERN LEAF IN BUTTON-LOOP STITCH.

THE engraving represents a particularly light and feathery fern-leaf of the blechnum species, and the working of the same is simplicity itself, and therefore is quite within the ability of a fairly-experienced embroiderer. The mid-rib is simulated by a line of crewel-stitch. The fronds are composed of a series of button-stitch loops made in precisely the same manner as the loops that often are put upon dresses to pass the hooks into; observe the buttonhole stitches all lie in the same direction, and to produce this effect it is necessary to hold the bottom of the leaf always towards you. Begin with the frond at the top of the right-hand side, bring up the needle and cotton close by the crewel-stitch rib in the place where you desire the loop to commence, insert the needle in the material at the distance of about a quarter of an inch to the right, and bring it up in the same place from whence it started, and draw through; do two more stitches in the same way and there will be three threads or strands whereon the buttonhole stitches are to be worked; do these as neatly and evenly as possible, and when the loop is nicely filled pass the needle to the back of the material at the top of the loop and bring it out beside the mid-rib in readiness for working another button-loop stitch a little lower than the one you have just completed, and continue similarly to the bottom of the right-hand side of the rib, and fasten

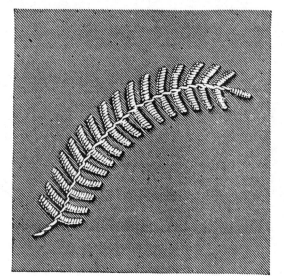

A Fern Leaf in Button-Loop Stitch.

off. Resume at the extreme top of the stem and make one button-loop stitch pointing upwards; then proceed down the left-hand side in loops to correspond with those on the right, but of course now bringing the needle and cotton up at the end of the loop furthest away from the mid-rib and inserting it in the material close by the rib, so as to preserve the required uniformity of the loops.

COMB AND BRUSH BAG.

A LIGHT and graceful design is shown on the front of this brush and comb bag, though it is only composed of bulrushes and reeds, and therefore while effective is very quickly worked. Our pattern bag takes half a yard of white satin jean, measuring 13 inches long and 9 inches in width across the centre, this 9 inches being reduced to 6½ inches by rounding the bag away top and bottom, and thus giving it an oval form. Cut two pieces of jean exactly alike; one for front and the other for back of bag, and having rounded them both to these measurements, cut out their edges in small scallops—a penny is a good guide for their size. Our design is worked only on the front of the bag, and consists of four bulrushes, all of about equal size, and of twelve or thirteen slender reeds; the number of either may, however, be entirely regulated according to the taste of the worker We advise her, if possible, to procure a bulrush as a guide, for it is infinitely easier to copy this stiff, curiously growing flower from a real one, though our description will be found very explicit. Work bulrush stems upwards, beginning at the bottom of the group, and use Strutt's No. 8 knitting cotton double, and make a "snail-trail" stitch stem, this stitch being illustrated in full size in No. 45 of "Weldon's Practical Needlework," which is devoted to Mountmellick work. To work snail-trail stitch bring up the cotton on the right side of the material on the traced line, hold the cotton under the thumb of the left hand, and passing the needle *over* the cotton held by the thumb, insert it in the material on the left-hand side of the line about one-eighth of an inch from where it was before brought up and bring it up on the opposite side of the traced line; it thus passes below the material and below the cotton held by the thumb and over the cotton that is threaded in the needle, draw through, and by this process a long straight stitch and a small loop stitch will be formed, again hold the cotton under the

4

thumb, and continue; the needle is set in only a very slightl slanting direction upon the guiding line. Stitch in *close* back stitching the oblong outline of the brown top or flower, and having thus clearly defined it cut No. 2 Strutt's knitting cotton into $\frac{1}{8}$-inch lengths (it will require a good many of these), and proceed to stitch each of these tiny lengths quite close together up the centre of the outlined flower until the whole is covered by them. Work the slender tip or st-m, which is at the top of the bulrushes, in a few fine crewel stitches, and then proceed to trim the coarse cotton, which is sewn down into shape, using a pair of *very* sharp scissors. Shape and trim these cottons to the outlined edge, and fray or split the soft cotton scraps a little, so as to get the soft, fluffy and rounded appearance of the

in the same way, and when the length of the bulrush is completed the mesh is drawn out, the cotton is fastened off, and another row is worked in the same manner quite close to the row that has just been done; when sufficient rug stitch is accomplished to cover the surface of the bulrush, the cotton is cut, and combed out and clipped to the shape desired. Bulrushes are also very properly worked in French knots, and sometimes in bullion stitch. The reeds in this group are all of them outlined in "snail-trail" stitch in No. 12 Strutt's knitting cotton, and in outlining the thicker ones use this cotton *double*. A very slender reed at the top of our group, running upwards between two bulrushes, is most effectively contrived, and this is done by working a close herringbone from side to side across the reed *over* the outlining. This has a pretty lace-like effect, and

Comb and Brush Bag.

bulrush, and also to hide the stitching by which it is sewn on. All the four bulrushes on this brush and comb bag are alike; so having done one according to these directions, copy it exactly, and reproduce in the other three here depicted. Rushes can also be executed in fluffy rug stitch, which is worked in a parallel direction from left to right, over a netting mesh about three-quarters of an inch wide, or a slip of stout cardboard cut to the same width will serve the purpose; bring up the needle and cotton on the outline of the bulrush on the right side of the material, hold the mesh upon the material, keeping it in place by pressure of the left-hand thumb, pass the cotton over the mesh, then under, and take two small stitches into the material to secure the loop. Every stitch is worked

is very suitable indeed for these slim, graceful reeds. We notice a slightly thickened reed to the left of this one, and this thickness is obtained by filling its centre up with a close row of French knots The manner of working these two reeds is repeated in all the others, so it seems unnecessary to detail them separately. Close, fine crewel stitch may be used to fill in the thicker reeds instead of the French knots, if preferred, as will be seen in one thick and short reed at the base of our group; but we prefer French knots as a filling, always advising the outlining of these reeds being entirely embroidered in "snail-trail" stitch. Join the two pieces of material together with a buttonhole serrated edge as illustrated and described in No. 45 of "Weldon's Practical Needlework," leaving the top of the bag open, and finish off with the usual knitted fringe. The button-holing should be worked in No. 12 Strutt's knitting cotton, and the fringe may be made of a coarser size, if preferred. Knitted fringe is illustrated in full working size, No. 45, of "Weldon's Practical Needlework Series." Wind a supply of No. 12 knitting cotton upon four separate balls and use from all four balls together, working with a pair of No. 11 steel knitting needles. Cast on 12 stitches. **1st row**—Make 1 (by passing all four strands of the cotton round

Pillow Sham.   Design of Hops, Blackberries, Butterflies, &c.

the needle), knit 2 together, knit 1, and repeat this three times. Every row is the same. When you have knitted a sufficient length to go nicely round the article you intend trimming, cast off 7 stitches, break off the cotton, and draw the end through the last stitch on the right-hand needle. Slip the 5 remaining stitches off the left-hand needle, and unravel them all the way along, and a pretty crinkled fringe will be produced. Sew the fringe by the loop stitches that are at the top of the heading to the edge of the buttonhole stitches that border the piece of Mountmellick embroidery. A fringe useful for trimming toilet sets and other articles of Mountmellick embroidery, for which a lighter and more open fringe is desired than the handsome, thick, crinkly fringe mentioned above, may be worked with either single or double cotton, and if the cotton

make 1, knit 2 together, knit 1. **2nd row**—Slip the first stitch, knit 6. Repeat these two rows alternately for the length required. When the mesh gets full of loops those at the end can be slipped off to make room for more. A twist is given to each loop by putting in a knitting pin and twisting the strands of cotton tightly one over the other, then draw the pin out, and the fringe is complete.

PILLOW SHAM.
DESIGN OF HOPS, BLACKBERRIES, BUTTERFLIES, &c.

OUR engraving represents a pillow sham beautifully embroidered in design of hops and leaves, blackberries, buds, flies, &c. Of course

Square for a Quilt. Anemones, Conventionally Treated.

be used double it is wound in two separate balls, then knit from the two balls together. Procure two skeins of Strutt's best knitting cotton, No. 6 or No. 8, and a pair of No. 11 or No. 12 steel knitting needles, also a bone netting mesh from one and a half inches to two inches wide to determine the depth of the fringe, or if a knitting mesh is not handy, a strip of very thick cardboard will answer equally well. Begin by casting on 7 stitches. **1st row**—Insert the needle in the first stitch in the usual manner, take the mesh and hold it between the thumb and first finger of the left hand close up to the work, and pass the cotton first along the back and then up the front of the mesh, and round the point of the right hand needle, and knit off the stitch, keeping it close to the mesh on which the loop of fringe is wound, knit plain the next stitch, make 1, knit 2 together,

every one is aware that a pillow sham is intended simply as an ornamental covering to spread over a bed pillow by day, and is removed at night. The idea comes from America, and is rapidly gaining ground in this country; everything that adds to the attractiveness of our rooms is a decided acquisition. It is usual to make a pillow sham several inches larger than the pillow over which it is to be spread. The size of our model is 30 inches by 24 inches; the material is white satin jean, and the embroidery is executed with Strutt's No 6 and No. 8 knitting cotton; the former is employed for the hops and blackberries, for most of the stems, the largest leaves, the bodies of the flies, and the buttonhole stitched scallops, and the latter for the remaining portions of the design. By referring to the engraving it will be seen that the embroidery in the upper left-hand corner corresponds with the embroidery in the lower right-hand corner, and also the embroidery in the upper right-hand corner with that in the lower left-hand corner; the centre of the pillow sham is occupied by a trailing spray of hops, blackberries, and leaves, with a butterfly, dragon fly, and moth hovering near. The hops are worked in buttonhole stitches grouped together, and they are shown in a large design, also fully detailed, in No. 45 of Weldon's "Practical Needlework." Short stitches are placed at the sides and long stitches in the centre of the loop; the bottom loop is worked first, and each successive loop laps slightly over its predecessor until the top of the hop is reached. The blackberries consist of French knots clustered together in a circle, large highly raised knots being used in the centre and smaller ones outside in crewel stitch veining, some with feather stitch and coral stitch; while others in addition to this filling are dotted round the outline with tiny French knots. All the tendrils are worked in snail-trail stitch. The wings of the butterfly are tastefully surrounded by an outline of cable-plait stitch and raised buttonhole stitches, the former on the front wings, the latter on the back wings, where also a little overcasting is introduced, as will be seen in the illustration; the spots on the wings are represented by circular clusters of tiny French knots, and the blotches by discs of worm stitches on the front wings, and by lobes of overcast stitch on the back wings; the body is effectively displayed by means of solid firm overcasting; two small French knots simulate eyes, the antennæ are crewel stitched, and terminate in a very tiny French knot: a few crewel stitches are

Square for a Quilt. Lilium Auratum, Conventionally Treated.

resemblance of the spherical shape of the natural berry. The buds are simulated in smooth satin stitch. The leaves are very variously worked; several are in Indian filling and several in feather stitch. A handsome spray of leaves will be noticed near the centre of the cloth; these are marginally outlined with raised satin stitch, the stitches being set quite evenly on the side nearest the centre of the leaf, and extending outwards more or less according as the leaf is more or less serrated; a line of crewel stitch and daisy loops in the middle of the leaf makes an effective mid-rib. Another pretty style of leaf is worked with an outline of raised buttonhole stitches and a mid-rib of crewel stitch, with branching veins of bullion stitches. Several leaves are defined with cable plait and filled, some with a used to depict lines of colour on the wings. The dragon fly has a body quite as long as that of the butterfly (about 2 inches long), but much thinner; it looks very natural in raised overcasting; the wings, of which there are two on each side, are represented in smooth satin stitch, the stitches meeting and forming a kind of streak down the middle of the wings; the antennæ consist of crewel stitch and French knots, which latter also are used to denote the eyes. The moth has a wide body, worked in much raised overcasting; its four wings are effected in feather stitch, the eyes in French knots, and the feelers in crewel stitch. When the Mountmellick embroidery is completed, the pillow sham is finished off with scallops of jagged buttonholing; the first buttonhole stitch is about half an inch long, and each successive stitch is shortened till six or seven stitches are worked, when do another long stitch like the first, and continue. The pillow sham may be trimmed with torchon lace put on full in the manner shown in the engraving, or with a knitted fringe, as preferred.

SQUARE FOR A QUILT.
ANEMONES, CONVENTIONALLY TREATED.

THIS anemone design matches splendidly with the conventional design of lilium auratum; in fact, the two subjects have been specially arranged in this form in order to be employed together for a quilt. It is so much handier to embroider a quilt in separate squares than in one large piece; each square can be put away when finished, and kept clean till the whole number are complete, when they will be sewn together, and bordered according to taste. The anemones are embroidered with Strutt's No. 8 knitting cotton, upon white satin jean, cut into squares measuring 18 inches across. The **Stem,** which you will observe is very erratic in its course, is worked throughout in the new stitch, called thorn stitch (see page 14); it lends itself admirably to graceful curves, and besides forming the stem, also passes as a mid-rib down the centre of all the leaves. Thorn stitch is a combination of coral stitch and French knots, and is pretty for stems of medium width, and also for the outlining of leaves and petals. Begin by tracing two parallel lines to denote the width the thorn stitch is required to be. Bring the needle and cotton out at the top midway between the two lines, hold the cotton under the left-hand thumb, insert the needle to take up five or six threads of material straight on the line to the left-hand side, and pass the point of the needle over the cotton held by the thumb and draw through; place the thumb again upon the cotton and make a similar stitch on the line on the right-hand side and draw through; both the stitches are set in perpendicularly, but the second stitch must be slightly lower than the first; a strand of cotton on the surface of the material connects the two stitches together, and so far the work is precisely identical with "Single Coral Stitch," Fig. 10, No. 45, "Weldon's Practical Needlework Series." But now comes the difference which effects such an improvement and transforms an otherwise simple stitch into a particularly ornamental one: Retaining the cotton again under the left-hand thumb, pass the point of the needle under the cotton, and over and under, and over and under the cotton again, keep the twist close on the needle and the cotton still under pressure of thumb and turn the point of the needle upwards and carry it over the strand that runs across from the first to the second stitch, and inserting it in the material, bring it out below the strand and midway between the lines and over the cotton held by the thumb, and draw through, being careful not to disarrange the twist, which when drawn up closely forms a knot. Continue working by the above instructions, and you will produce a stem of thorn stitch as represented in the engraving. The **Leaves** are characterised by their large size and jagged outline. The leaf in the right-hand bottom corner is margined in buttonhole stitch, the stitches being mostly of the same length, and so placed as to fall nicely into the contour of the tracing; an elaborate decoration consisting of rows of stars composed of four daisy-loop stitches, set round a tiny French knot, is carried up each side of the leaf between the mid-rib and the outline. A leaf at the bottom of the square is simply delineated with snail-trail stitch, and veinings of bullion stitches branch out on both sides from the mid-rib. An effective leaf on the left-hand side is worked in buttonhole stitch on the *lower* half of each indentation; the stitches are at a little distance one from the other, the spike of each stitch pointing towards the outside of the leaf, and to get from the extreme end of a line of buttonhole stitch into the place for commencing the next line you will carry a few crewel stitches along the upper half of each indentation—a glance at the engraving will show what is meant; the interior of the leaf, between the jagged outline and the mid-rib, is fairly well filled with good-sized French knots. The bold leaf in the centre of the design is executed with very little trouble; it is outlined with a wide margin of satin stitches of graduated length, and then decorated with ten studs or knobs ranged in two rows, five studs in a row, on each side of the mid-rib. A smaller leaf at the top of the square is also easily accomplished by employing French knots for the outline and crewel stitch for the veining. The anemone **Flowers** are very handsome when nicely worked; perhaps the fully developed flower

at the top of the design is the most taking, as seen in the engraving, but the others are really quite as effective. Each flower comprises ten petals. We will first of all consider the topmost flower; here the five back petals are embroidered in satin stitch, and these are considerably wider than the front petals, which, after being carefully outlined with cable plait, are decorated with a diamond filling, cross stitches, and French knots; the seed vessel in the centre of the flower is admirably represented by many French knots clustered together in a circle, rather large knots being in the middle and smaller ones outside to produce a spherical appearance. The flower on the left-hand side of the square has five petals conspicuously in

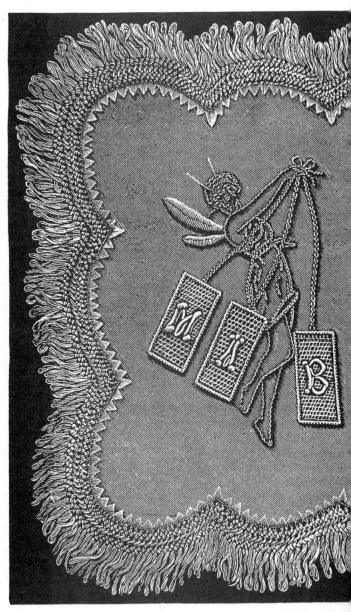

Figure Subjec

front, and beautifully outlined with saw-tooth buttonholing, with a rib of cable plait running perpendicularly up the centre of each; the five back petals are nothing more than lozenge-shaped blocks of smooth, perpendicular satin stitches, imitating, as it were, merely the tips of the actual petals; then a cluster of French knots in the centre of the flower will successfully imitate the seed vessel. Another flower on the right-hand side of the design corresponds in size and shape with the one we have just described, the only difference is in the working of the five front petals, which here possess a perpendicular rib of coral stitch, and are defined with bullion stitches placed in pairs vertically. Two buds are embroidered in their widest parts in rather a novel manner by twining a thread of cotton up and down in zig-zag fashion, and retaining it in position by a small stitch at each curve; the finer outline is executed in snail-trail stitch. The other buds are effected in satin stitch and crewel stitch. All the other squares that are required to make up the quilt must, of course, be traced to correspond with the foregoing; but the embroidery may be varied by introducing different combinations of stitches into the different squares, and this will exercise the ingenuity of the worker and at the same time add to the attractiveness of the quilt.

Pillow Sham.

SQUARE FOR QUILT.

Lilium Auratum, Conventionally Treated.

This handsome square, with its embroidery of lilies conventionally treated. is intended to be used with the anemone square represented on opposite page; the two should be sewn alternately together, and the seams covered with ornamental stitching, or bands of guipure insertion may be arranged to run between the squares, or squares of open guipure may be placed between the embroidered squares; whichever style is adopted the result will make a most artistic quilt.

The work is executed with Strutt's No. 8 knitting cotton, upon squares of the best white satin jean, each square measuring 18 inches across. The number of squares that have to be worked will depend entirely upon the size the quilt is required to be, and whether or not any guipure is used in addition to the satin jean. The quilt may be finished with a Mountmellick scalloped border, with knitted fringe, or with wide guipure lace. Begin by enlarging the lily design to the required size and trace it on the material. Then consider the **Stem**, the main portion of which is worked in cable plait, and the finer parts in snail-trail stitch and single thread couching. Next, observe the manipulation of the **Flowers**. The large flower in the centre of the square has all its petals outlined with the new thorn stitch, and in places where the tips of the petals are curved the work changes to over-casting, while certain coloured spots that appear upon the petals of the natural flower of the lilium auratum species are simulated by a rather close powdering of small daisy loops; the stamens are of crewel stitch, and these each are surmounted with an anther, the size and shape of a grain of rice, worked in highly raised satin stitch. In the bottom right-hand corner will be seen another flower very similar in size and shape to the one just described, but in this the petals are defined with cable plait, and their interiors filled with **V** stitches—*i.e.*, two spike stitches diverging at the top and thence meeting in a point over which a small straight stitch is set. Both flowers possess at their base two broad leaves embroidered in simple flat satin stitch. The semi-opened flower, or **blossom**, at the top of the spray, is outlined with cording stitch and closely margined with French knots; four good-sized studs or knobs of raised satin stitch decorate the centre of the middle petal, and the three stamens which emerge from this petal are worked in snail-trail stitch with small spots of raised satin stitch for anthers. Another blossom on the opposite side of the square is prettily embroidered with indented buttonhole stitch, the dents being turned towards the interior of the petals and the loops falling on the margin; the petals then are all filled more or less closely with French knots, as will be understood by consulting the engraving. A **bud** near the top of the spray begins with two points of neat feather stitch, and these merge together and the work changes into Indian filling covering the surface of the bud, which then is outlined with a couched thread, the same being passed down the centre nearly to the base, where the seed pot is represented by raised satin stitch; the long narrow leaf adjacent to this bud is worked in opus plumarium; the larger leaf is defined with cable plait, and its interior is filled with trellis, as shown in leaf on page 14. A small bud on the right-hand side of the square is embroidered throughout in close feather stitch excepting the seed vessel, which is raised satin stitch. Close by will be seen a thin leaf outlined with chain stitch, and possessing a mid-rib of open feather stitch. A sprig of four pretty **leaves** at the bottom of the square demands a little mention; the largest of these is elegantly fashioned in two sections, or divisions, that to the left being entirely occupied with Indian filling, that to the right with buttonstitch loops, as shown in full working size by Fig. 11 in sampler of leaves given in No. 69, "Weldon's Practical Needlework Series." A description of the small leaf with the dotted line of French knots will be found (Fig. 9) on the sampler; the pretty leaf at the end of the sprig is composed of bullion stitches worked in pairs extending from a mid-rib of crewel stitch, and the remaining leaf is worked in smooth satin stitch. On a stem couched with thick cotton, almost in the centre of the square, there is a leaf worked partly in raised overcasting and partly in trellis and cross stitches; also a smaller leaf with outline of saw-tooth buttonholing and a mid-rib of chain stitch. To the left of this is a sprig of three good-sized leaves; the largest is outlined with thorn stitch, and is richly veined with crewel stitch. The next consists entirely of worm stitches as leaf 10 on the sampler, in No. 69 of "Weldon's Practical Needlework," and the other resembles leaf 12 on the same sampler. Below the last-mentioned sprig another sprig of three leaves is observable, one of which consists of close feather-stitching outlined with a margin of French knots. The second is delineated with and has a mid-rib of crewel stitch, the veinings being of *point de reprise;* while the other, which is the smallest, is embroidered on one side with daisy loops, and on the opposite side between a mid-rib of chain stitch and an outline of crewel stitch there runs a row of tiny French knots. Point de reprise is familiar to workers of point lace, and is also used a good deal in drawn thread embroidery, but in case any of our readers may be ignorant of the procedure we will

10

here explain the method of working : Commence by forming four long stitches, close together and smooth and even one with another, like long satin stitches, across from side to centre of the leaf ; these long stitches have no occasion to appear at all on the back of the material, for by taking up a few threads of the material close against and level with the outline they may stretch from side to side on the surface only. Now having the needle and cotton on the right side of the work, take the needle over the first two of the long threads and under the second two, and draw through, turn the needle the reverse way and pass it over the two threads it just went under, and under the two threads it before went over, and draw through, and continue this in-and-out darning until the bar is well covered with stitches, never taking the needle through the material but only over and under the threads ; and proceed in the same manner with the

three tablets suspended from its hands by means of ribbons ; the tablets each bear one of the initials of the owner's name. On the other side, near the bottom corner, is a device something in the shape of a draped curtain band. If the owner possesses a crest it should be embroidered in this corner, above the band, taking, in fact, the place which here is occupied by a flower. On looking at the engraving you may be inclined to say, " This is an easy subject to undertake, there is not much work in it." You will be mistaken, there may not be a great deal to look at, for the material is by no means covered, but what there is is *fine work*, executed with fine cotton, and with the greatest neatness and exactness.

The model measures 26 inches by 18 inches. The best quality white satin jean is used for the foundation, and the embroidery is worked with Strutt's No. 12 knitting cotton, of which almost a

Tray Cloth. Design of Fuchsias.

other bars successively. An expert worker will be able to introduce different arrangements of stitches into various leaves so that all the squares required to make a quilt need not be an exact reproduction of the first square. The sampler giving twenty varieties for working leaves, as illustrated in No. 69, and the group of lilies, shown in No. 47 of " Woldon's Practical Needlework Series " will offer many ideas for varying the working of this handsome design.

PILLOW SHAM. FIGURE SUBJECT.

THE pillow sham from which our engraving is taken is embroidered in a novel, elegant, and highly original design. On the left-hand side we see a figure, with wings and arms outstretched, carrying

pound will be required as the fringe takes a quantity. Enlarge the design to the dimension stated, and trace it properly upon the material. The **Figure**—The head and body, arms, legs, and feet are delineated in crewel-stitch outline ; a belt, margined with chain stitch and decorated with studs of small French knots, passes round the waist. The wings are embroidered in Indian frilling, taking the stitches over and under one side and over and under the other side alternately, so that the stitches meet in the centre and form a kind of depressed rib. The tablets are shaped very similarly to a child's school slate ; parallelograms of close, even cable-plait stitch effect very good representations of frames. An initial letter is embroidered in highly-raised satin stitch in the centre of each tablet, and the remaining surface is then entirely filled with a network of honeycomb stitch, as see Fig. 32, No. 45.

"Weldon's Practical Needlework Series;" the ribbons upon which the tablets are suspended are delineated by lines of chain stitching, and these are apparently gathered up together in the hands and tied to simulate a bow, which bow is rendered in snail-trail stitch. The **Device**—The band is one and a quarter inches in width, and consists of four parallel rows of cable plait worked very finely and evenly at a little distance one from the other, thus there are three spaces available for decoration; the two outer spaces are embroidered with double feather-stitching, and the centre space is studded at regular intervals with medium-sized French knots; space is allowed at each end of the band to admit a curl or curve of the central part of the pattern to be placed, as shown in the engraving. A shield is thrown across the centre of the band, its outline is worked in highly raised overcasting; the criss-cross and the loop in the centre are composed of bullion stitches, and then the whole remaining interior of the shield is filled in closely with a powdering of French knots. The large ivy leaves at each end of the band are embroidered to match the shield,

TRAY CLOTH. DESIGN OF FUCHSIAS.

A FASHIONABLE tray cloth of oval shape, measuring 25 inches long by 18 inches wide, is beautifully worked in a lovely design of fuchsias, grouped in sprays as in a wreath. The sprays at first sight appear as if carelessly tied together, but if you look closely into the engraving you will see they really are most carefully arranged, for two distinct sprays, in which every one of the ten fuchsias and accompanying leaves and buds are embroidered in a different style, are placed upon one side of the cloth, and these are duplicated and repeated on the opposite side, so that the sprays correspond, and the left-hand side of the one comes opposite the right-hand side of the other, and *vice-versâ*.

The materials required are a piece of white satin jean sufficiently large to take the design, and a pound of Strutt's No. 10 knitting cotton. A good deal of cotton is consumed in knitting the fringe. The design must be enlarged from the engraving to the requisite size, and when it is properly sketched upon tracing cloth, or even

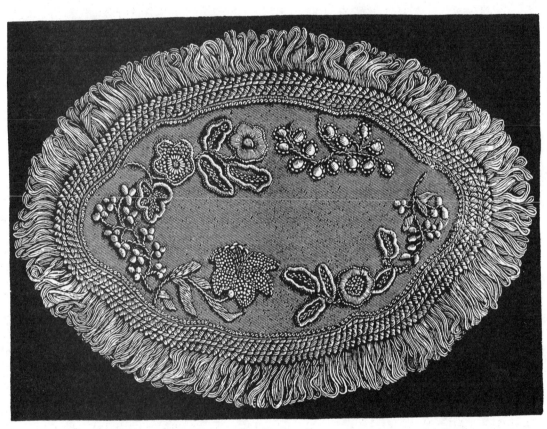

Toilet Mat.

but here some parts of the outline overcasting are much more prominent than other parts, and this is effected by putting in extra padding and taking wider stitches. The flower in the centre of the device is similarly worked, and it has eight bullion stitches rising in the centre and radiating upon the surface of the flower, which greatly add to its good appearance. Tiny sprays of leaves occupy part of the space between the band and the flower. There now remain the ten diamonds to be embroidered below the band, and then the device will be completed; these have their outline defined with raised overcasting, and a cross composed of two bullion stitches decorates the centre of each. The pillow-sham is edged with large scallops of raised buttonhole stitching, consisting of a series of stitches of graduated lengths forming angular points, as will be seen by consulting the engraving. It then is trimmed with knitted fringe.

on a large sheet of paper, it may easily be transferred to the material in readiness for working. Useful instructions for enlarging and transferring designs will be found on page 4, No. 47, "Weldon's Practical Needlework Series." An endless variety of stitches are employed in the embroidery of this handsome cloth. The thick **Stems** are in cable-plait, the narrower stems in snail-trail stitch, and the narrowest of all in crewel stitch. The **Bows**, by which the groups of sprays are apparently tied together, are worked, one in wide slanting cording stitch, and the other in cable plait. The fuchsias are embroidered in ten different ways, but of course the stamens admit of very little variation, and are for the most part formed of crewel stitch, with one small French knot at the end of each stamen to simulate the anther. We will describe the fuchsias in rotation, commencing on the left-hand side. The first fuchsia has the outline of the sepals worked simply in cable plait, a few long satin stitches simulate the inner petals; the calyx is represented by long, close buttonhole stitches, and the ovary or seed vessel being covered with a network of threads crossing each other in chessboard fashion, is completed with an outline of couching. **Second Fuchsia**—The sepals are entirely composed of good-sized French knots, the petals are worked in satin stitch, the calyx is prettily decorated with longitudinal twisted stitches, and the ovary is of solid raised overcasting. **Third Fuchsia**—The sepals are very elegantly effected in Indian filling ; the petals, which are more clearly visible than in either of the preceding flowers, are outlined with snail-trail stitch and dotted with French knots ; a mid-rib of crewel stitch from which small worms worked in pairs branch out on either side, constitutes a tasteful calyx, and a circle of French knots makes a good representation of an ovary. **Fourth Fuchsia**—The outline of the sepals is here delineated by cording stitch, and the petals are produced by doing rows of small neat back stitching, the calyx is raised overcasting, and the ovary is formed by satin stitches slanting crossways from side to side. **Fifth Fuchsia** (on the left-hand side of the bow outside the spray)—The sepals are executed entirely of French knots thickly

space between the buttonhole stitches of the preceding row, and thus the pairs of buttonhole stitches in every row alternate with each other, and a pretty dice-patterned network is produced as shown in the engraving. **Eighth Fuchsia**—The sepals are outlined with a neat firm couching and decorated with a row of small French knots, the tips of the petals are delineated by cable plait, the calyx is embroidered in wide overcasting, and a group of French knots represents the ovary. **Ninth Fuchsia**—This has its sepals worked in trellis stitch ; the petals are formed of several rows of chain stitch worked closely together in an upright position, buttonhole loops alternated with bars of satin stitch make a particularly pretty calyx, and the ovary is produced in flat satin stitch. **Tenth Fuchsia**—The sepals are executed in slightly raised overcasting, not any petals are visible ; an elegant calyx is formed by a series of bullion stitches or worms stretching across from side to side, and overcasting is used for the ovary. The **Buds** need not be minutely described ; some are worked in feather stitch, some in satin stitch, but all are in solid embroidery ; not any of the buds

Round Toilet Mat. Lily and Leaves.

studded together, the petals and also the calyx are of smooth close satin stitch, and the ovary is of raised satin stitch. **Sixth Fuchsia** (on the right-hand side of the bow outside the spray)— The sepals each have a mid-rib of couching from which daisy loops project on either side, the petals are outlined with chain stitch, the calyx is covered entirely with laid threads couched as in diaper darning, and the ovary is studded with small back stitching. **Seventh Fuchsia**—The sepals are embroidered with close feather stitch ; very pretty petals are produced in *point de Sorrento* ; the calyx consists of worms set perpendicularly, and the ovary is of solid raised overcasting. Point de Sorrento is executed in rows backwards and forwards—in the first row you work the buttonhole stitches into the material, putting two stitches closely together, then leaving a little space, and doing two more stitches, and so on ; but in the following rows, after beginning by steadying the turn of the row into the material close against the outline, you will form each pair of buttonhole stitches upon the thread that extends along the

are outlined. Many of the **Leaves** can be identified among the engravings of leaves worked in full actual size, as shown by Figs. 1 to 20 in No. 69 of this Work Series, and need not be again described in this place ; the early issues, Nos. 45, 47, 50, 69, and 79 of the series contain examples of leaves in considerable variety ; in fact, there is here great scope for the ingenuity of a clever worker, and every known stitch may be brought into use in the form of outline or filling.

This tray cloth is margined with an edge of wide buttonhole stitch ; the satin jean is then cut to shape and a knitted fringe is sewn on.

THREE TOILET MATS.

TOILET mats being always a useful addition to a dressing table, we think the three we now present to the notice of our workers may find favour, more especially perhaps in the eyes of those housewives who prefer mats to a toilet cover, which though it protects, effectually conceals a handsomely polished duchesse table. This large oval centre mat, on page 11, is 14 inches long and 8 inches across its widest part, being slightly scalloped all round to define its shape. The pair of small octagon-shaped mats are each cut out of a piece of white satin jean, about 6 inches in diameter. The flowers embroidered on these mats are lilies and geraniums, also there are some grapes, and leaves with a few berries, and bits of shamrock. These are all alike worked both finely and closely, and not much padded, as the flatter they are when on a table the better for the security of any ornaments which may be placed upon them. Use the best white satin jean at 27 inches wide, and Strutt's knitting cotton, Nos. 12 and 14, also Bartleet's Mountmellick needles. The chief stitches introduced in these developments are snail trail, French knots, buttonhole, and a close-cording stitch, which latter adapts itself exactly to the long, slender, straight leaves of the lilies wherever they occur. The lily on the oval mat is outlined in a fine herring-bone stitch, and filled in very closely with a series of

surface by a lily group, the lily being outlined in fine snail-trail stitch, and filled in exactly like its fellow on the large mat which we have just described. The six leaves are effectively worked in cording stitch, and there are also some bits of grass simulated by worms branching from fine stems of crewel stitch. On the fellow small mat, illustrated on page 13, is grouped a bunch of grapes, a vine leaf, and many snail-trail tendrils; the vine leaf is outlined with French knots and veined with coral or feather stitch, and the grapes are all embroidered in satin stitch, and their stems in crewel stitch. Worm stitch, also known as "twisted stitch," "bullion," "roll picot," or "point de minute," is worked thus: Bring up the needle and cotton close to the upper side of a crewel stitch, insert the needle at a distance of about half an inch or three-eighths of an inch above the line of crewel stitching in the direction you wish the "worm" to lie when finished, and passing it along the back of the material, bring out the point in the place the cotton springs from, and now carefully and evenly wind the cotton eight or nine times

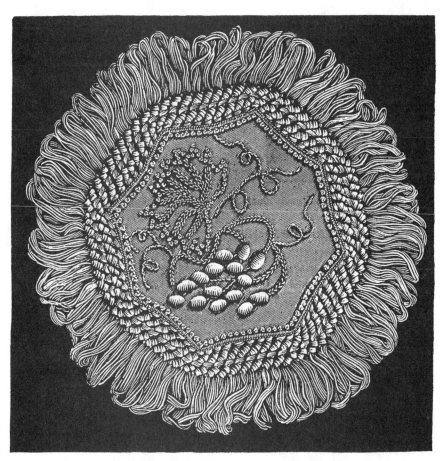

Round Toilet Mat. Vine and Leaves.

small French knots, having a few stamens worked in crewel stitch and each stamen tipped with a tiny worm to represent a seedling. The geraniums, of which there are three on the oval mat, are worked with a little variety. That above the lily a trifle to the left, has an outline in braid stitch, and each petal or scallop filled with French knots, and a centre of small worms radiating from a tiny middle. The geranium immediately above the lily is buttonholed in long satin stitches from a very *small* satin-stitched centre to the edge of the flower; the third geranium, which is on the right of the lily, has a *large* centre clustered with French knots, and a narrow buttonholed edge. The geranium leaves are all alike, narrowly buttonholed all round their edges, and veined or centred with fine crewel stitch. The shamrock leaves at the left-hand side of mat are satin stitched with snail-trail stems. The grapes are worked in satin stitch, surrounded with tiny French knots, and the stems are snail-trail stitch. One of the small mats, on page 12, is nearly covered over its whole

closely round the needle with the right hand, while you hold the needle steadily in position by pressure of the left-hand thumb, and thus you will see the length of the stitch is regulated by the amount of material taken on the needle, which is equivalent to the length the "worm" will be when finished; keep the left-hand thumb pressing firmly on the roll of stitches while you draw the needle and cotton through the material and also through the roll of stitches, then gently pull the cotton upwards till the "worm" lies smoothly on the surface of the material, when pass the needle to the back of the work where it was before put in at the top of the stitch, and bring it to the front again by the line of crewel stitching in readiness for commencing the next stitch. All the "worm" stitches are manipulated in this manner. It is no consequence whether you work from right to left or from left to right, the important thing is to retain the left-hand thumb firmly pressing upon the roll of stitches until the cotton is quite drawn through;

A Leaf worked in Thorn Stitch, Trellis, and French Knots.

LEAF: THORN STITCH, TRELLIS, AND FRENCH KNOTS.

An effective leaf outlined in the new Thorn stitch, is illustrated here. The surface of the material within the thorn-stitched outline is decorated by a trellis work of threads carried across the leaf

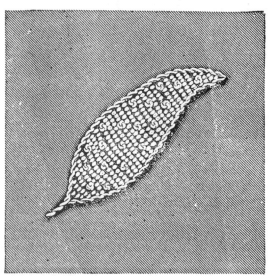

A Leaf in Solid Work of Spot Stitch and French Knots.

slanting vertically from side to side, three threads in one direction and two threads in the opposite direction; and in places where these threads cross each other little groups of four French knots are dotted together, doing one knot in each of the angles, or corners, of the trellis. This leaf is bold in style, and well adapted for placing in large pieces of work.

LEAF: SOLID WORK OF SPOT STITCH AND FRENCH KNOTS.

HERE is a leaf embroidered throughout in solid work, and is very useful to blend with other leaves of a lighter character. The outline is delineated by crewel stitch; and within this the entire surface of the centre of the leaf is filled with spot stitches interspersed here and there with French knots; the spot stitches are very simply formed by working two or three tiny back stitches one over the other, but care must be taken to place them with regularity, almost quite close together, in the manner which will be clearly understood by consulting the engraving.

POWDERING.

THIS charming manner of elaborating any large piece of Mountmellick work is not only novel, but most effective, as, when evenly and carefully worked, these little "worms," or "grubs," as some of our readers prefer to call them, assist materially in throwing up into relief a good design, and give an air of "finish" to the whole.

The engraving shows the "worms" in half size, and to ensure the

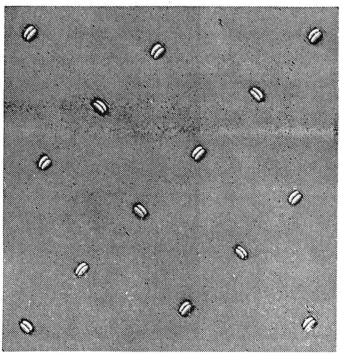

Powdering.

evenness of this powdering, after having traced on jean any design you propose embroidering, make tiny *dots* exactly two inches apart slantwise across the material, and each dot serves as a mark whereon to embroider a couple of "worms," each pair of "worms" being worked alternately—one pair uprightly, the next pair crossways, and so on until the material is sufficiently covered with powdering.

To make these "worms" the worker must first bring needle and cotton up on the surface of her material, and then re-insert it about a quarter of an inch distant, bringing it up again through the first hole, keeping the cotton rather loose; then twist the cotton nine times round the needle and put the needle down through the second hole, drawing the cotton tightly, and you thus have a neat, tight little "worm;" do another in the same way close beside it, and then fasten the thread off very firmly at the back of material, beginning afresh on the next dot for another pair of "worms."

We advise our workers to quite finish the entire embroidering of any design, leaving this powdering until quite the last, as in the case of any of these "worms" coming in the way of or through the flowers they must be omitted and continued where they can be worked without interfering at all with the pattern, to which this powdering is quite subservient. No. 12 Strutt's knitting cotton is a good useful size for embroidering "worms," using a No. 4 needle

[86]

The Priscilla Needlework Book

For 1904
Price, 10 Cents

Published by The Priscilla Publishing Company
Boston, Massachusetts

The Priscilla Needlework Book

For 1904

Price   .   .   10 Cents

Published by
The Priscilla Publishing Company, Boston, Massachusetts
Copyrighted, 1903

MOUNTMELLICK EMBROIDERY

THE genuine Mountmellick embroidery is always white cotton thread upon white satin jean or heavy linen. Very pretty work in blue and white or red upon a white foundation, in the designs and stitches peculiar to the style, is very often sold under this name, but it is not correct. The name is also incorrectly applied to embroidery in silk or crewel on a woollen foundation for children's garments. This is simply an extension of the style to larger uses than attempted by the originators.

A very strong, firm satin jean is now manufactured expressly for the embroidery. The thread used is a rather coarse embroidery or knitting-cotton of moderate twist, one number being usually retained throughout a design, although in some cases two, or even three, are employed, according to the effect desired. Tapestry or large-eyed carpet needles are needed. They must pull the thread through the material without dragging.

The designs are bold and free, with open spacing ; mostly

No. 603. Table Cover in Mountmellick Embroidery. Lilies and Passion Flowers.
Perforated pattern, 34 x 20 inches, 50 cents.   Stamped on white satin jean, 75 cents.   Cotton for working, $1.75 additional.

The embroidery is a strong, durable, and handsome work. When formed of the proper materials, it is almost indestructible, and will endure for generations. It is eminently suitable for coverlets, pillow-shams, toilet covers, drapery for bed, toilet table, and windows, and for smaller articles, as nightdress sachets, comb and brush bags, doilies, pincushions, and covers for bedroom candle stands. Indeed, almost any article of drapery for a chamber may be carried out in this very beautiful and unique style of embroidery. The pure white tone and the artistic excellence of the designs, combined with the novelty of the conventional treatment, render the work particularly attractive. Although it soils easily, it may be as easily laundered.

floral, and retaining the natural shape, but strongly conventionalized by the peculiar stitches. Certain favorite designs have been repeated for such a long period that they have become characteristic of the style. Such are the passion-flower and the lily, the wild rose and morning-glory, the maiden-hair fern, blackberries, oak leaves and acorns, ferns and wheat, and the shamrock. These designs are stamped as for ordinary embroidery. Many floral designs are suitable for Mountmellick work.

There is yet another peculiarity about this embroidery, and that lies in the method of finishing each article, whatever its nature or purpose. The edge is invariably buttonholed around in one of the many ways, and it is often further finished with

3

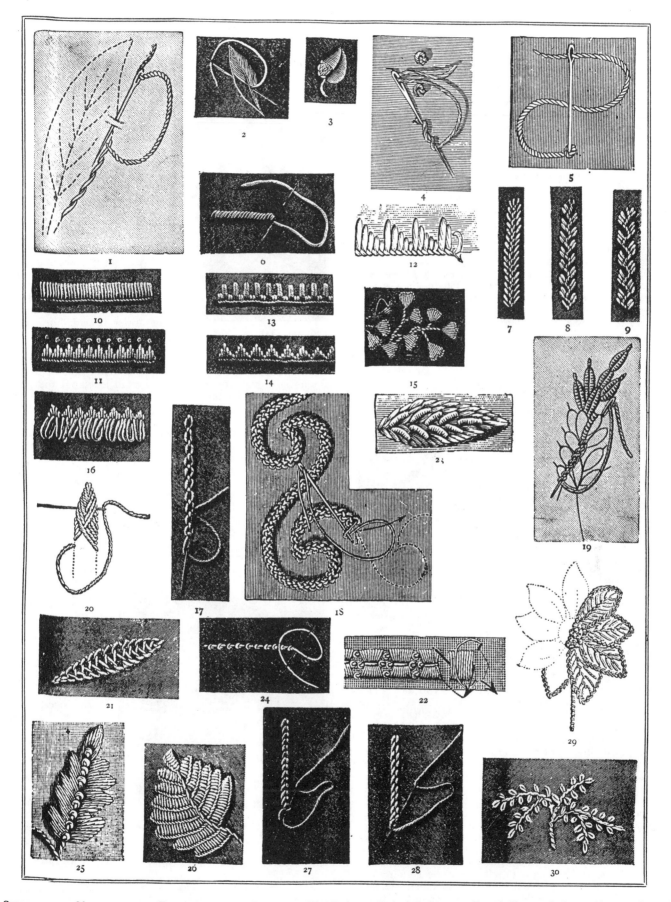

STITCHES FOR MOUNTMELLICK EMBROIDERY. — 1, Outline. 2, Flat Satin. 3, Raised Satin. 4, 5, French Knots. 6, Overcasting. 7, 8, 9, Feather. 10, 11, 12, 13, 14, Buttonhole Stitch for Borders. 15, Fern in Buttonhole Stitch. 16, Looped Buttonhole Stitch for Border. 17, Cable. 18, Cable Plait. 19, Way of Working Wheat in Bullion Stitch. 20, Leaf Stitch. 21, Leaf Worked in Trellis Stitch. 22, Border. 23, Leaf in Satin and Bullion Stitch. 24, Snail. 25, Leaf in Satin and Snail Stitch. 26, Leaf Worked in Buttonhole Stitch. 27, Chain. 28, Cording. 29, Flower Worked in Herring-bone Stitch and French Knots. 30, Leaf Stitch for Small Spray.

a fringe knit from the same cotton thread. The stitches employed may be traced to various sources; many of them being such as are used in ordinary embroidery, while others may be traced to ancient pieces of German needlework. The well-known outline, stem, crewel or Kensington stitch, plays an important part in each piece of embroidery. So also do satin-stitch, both flat and raised, French knots, split, overcasting, dot, feather and chain stitches, couching, and the universal buttonhole-stitch. These are so well known as to need no detailed description, except to say that in split-stitch the method is similar to crewel or stem stitch, except that the needle is brought up through the thread; hence the name "split." In raised satin-stitch (Fig. 3, page 4), some workers use small tufts of cotton wool as a foundation, but in the best Mountmellick embroidery the relief is given by closely set darned stitches. The latter launders much better and is much more durable than the former.

Outline, split, and overcasting are used to outline petals of flowers, leaves, and for stems and veins, and feather and chain stitches for veins. French knots and dot-stitch, which is simply isolated back-stitches, are used as well as satin-stitch for filling in leaves and petals. Chain-stitch is not in common use in Mountmellick work, although it is often placed as a padding under overcasting or satin-stitches for stems; or, when a leaf requires to be higher in the middle than elsewhere, then chain-stitch is worked over the darning and then covered. Couching is used in its simplest form. Four or five or more strands of cotton are sewn at intervals with a straight stitch. It is used principally for veins, stalks, and straight lines.

FIG. 31. EXAMPLE OF MOUNTMELLICK WORK

Buttonhole-stitch plays a very important part in this style of embroidery, besides its use as a finishing agent, and may be worked in a very great many different ways. The fronds of a maiden-hair fern and several fancy edges are given in the illustrations. The stitch is used for petals of roses and for other flowers, and sometimes for leaves. When working an edge, it is a good plan to run a few darning-stitches along the lower outline to give solidity to the work. Indented buttonholing consists of sets of six or more stitches of graduated lengths worked on a straight line, as shown in Fig. 14. In saw-tooth buttonholing (Fig. 13) there are two long and two short stitches. Sometimes a straight row of detached French knots is added at the top of the stitches, making a very easy yet effective finish, as shown in Fig. 11. Looped buttonhole-stitch makes a pretty edge for small pieces of work.

The scroll-like border design, Fig. 18, is in cable-plait-stitch, a highly ornamental and closely twisted stitch, much used for stems and for outlining bold, conventional designs. Before attempting this, it would be well to master simple cable-stitch (Fig. 17), one of the most beautiful and popular of the Mountmellick stitches. The cut shows a simple stitch which is quickly worked, although the explanation makes it appear very complicated. Cable-stitch (Fig. 17) is worked vertically. Bring up the needle on the right side of the material, hold the cotton straight down under the left thumb, pass the needle from right to left under the cotton so held down, and draw it up till the cotton held under the thumb is a small loop, then keeping the thumb in the same position, insert the point of the needle in the material below the cotton, and just underneath where you before brought it out, bring

the point of the needle in a straight line a quarter of an inch below, but *not* to pass through the loop of cotton that is still held under the thumb. Release the thumb, and draw the loop of cotton closely round the top of the needle and pass the cotton from left to right under the point, and draw the needle at once through the little loop at the top and through this present loop, and the stitch is made. Repeat indefinitely. The effect is of a small knot of cotton linking one chain with another. Be careful always to pull the cotton closely round the top of the needle, and to keep it under the point, before drawing up.

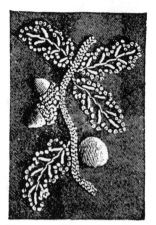

FIG. 32. OAK LEAVES AND ACORNS

When learning to work cable-plait-stitch (Fig. 18), prepare two parallel lines, by stamping or drawing threads, about a quarter of an inch apart, and begin on the left-hand side to work from left to right. Bring up the needle and cotton on the lower tracing-line, hold the cotton down under the left thumb and pass the needle from right to left under the cotton so held, and draw up till the cotton still held under the thumb is brought to the size of a small loop, put the point of the needle under the small loop, raising the loop level with the top tracing-line, where insert the needle, bringing out the point straight below on the bottom tracing-line, release the loop from under the thumb and draw it round the top of the needle, and pass the cotton thence from left to right under the point of the needle and draw through. Every stitch is formed in this same way, and the result produces a raised thick plait on the right side of the material, and a series of small perpendicular stitches on the wrong. Practice will render this stitch quite easy; but as a small knot is formed in the cotton by the process of working, it is almost impossible to undo when once formed, great attention must be paid to twisting the cotton rightly, and to keeping the stitches the same even width along the line. The edge of a cloth with this border is finished with dog-tooth buttonholing and the characteristic knitted fringe.

Bullion-stitch (Fig. 19), or "worms," is another extremely popular in Mountmellick work, and enters largely into flowers, leaves, wheat ears, and sprays. It resembles French knots, but is made long and narrow instead of round, and is worked in the same general way. Leaves in this stitch may be worked in two different ways, composed entirely of the "worms," or with the centre only filled in (Fig. 23).

FIG. 33. BLACKBERRIES, FLOWERS, AND LEAVES

There are several stitches that through constant use have come to be peculiar to Mountmellick work. Of these, snail-stitch (Fig. 24) is easily worked, and is as effective as some of the more difficult ones. It is used for midribs, tendrils, and outlines of larger leaves. It is worked with the line held towards you, or from right to left. The thread is held down over the outline with the left thumb and a small stitch made in the stuff under the thread on the outline toward the right side. The thread must be kept under the needle and the stitch drawn up tightly. The effect of snail-stitch varies greatly according to whether the separate stitches are near together or far apart. The methods of making chain, cording, and bullion stitches are readily seen in the cuts.

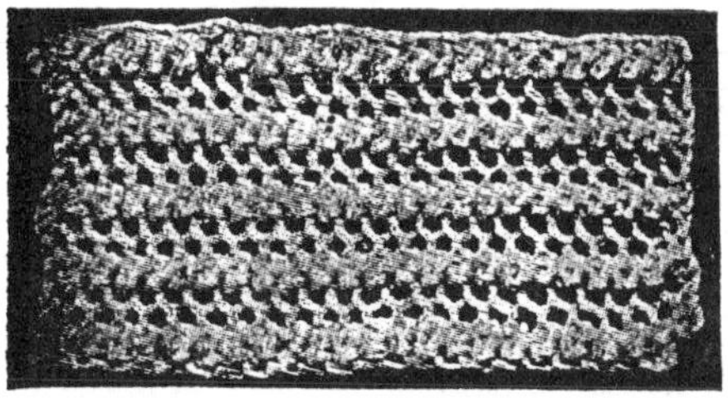

FIG. 34. KNITTED INSERTION FOR MOUNT-
MELLICK WORK

Figure 31, page 5, shows in reduced form a very good example of true Mountmellick embroidery. The method of working, and the stitches employed, are very clearly illustrated. Flat satin-stitch is employed for the pansies and for the star-flowers. On the larger petals of the pansies the long satin-stitches are caught down by two rows of short stitches. This adds both durability and beauty to the work. The centres are worked in satin-stitch, while the markings of the flower are done in stem-stitch. The edges of the leaves are done in buttonhole, and the centres in feather-stitch. The different stitches are so well portrayed in the cut that no further explanation is needed.

The fringe is shown in Fig. 36, page 6, and is knit of No. 12 knitting-cotton, using the thread of four separate balls as one strand, with No. 11 steel needles. Cast on 12 stitches. 1st row — Make 1 by passing all four strands of cotton round the needle; knit 2 together, knit 1, and repeat three times. Every row the same. When sufficient length is knit to go loosely around the article, cast off 7 stitches, break off the cotton and draw the end through the last stitch on the right-hand needle. Slip the 5 remaining stitches off the left needle

and unravel them all the way along. This produces a pretty crinkled fringe. The more tightly the knitting has been done, the more wavy will be the fringe, though, of course, this effect is lost the first time the work is washed. Sew the fringe to the edge of the buttonhole-stitch that borders the piece of embroidery.

Sometimes bedspreads are made of squares or strips of sateen or linen, embroidered with Mountmellick sprays set together with an insertion, knit as for the fringe, but not ravelled out. This insertion is shown in Fig. 34, page 6. A deep fringe finishes the whole spread. Laid over a colored slip, such a coverlet has a lighter and richer appearance than one of solid material.

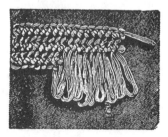

FIG. 35. DETAIL OF NIGHTDRESS CASE, NO. 99-3-1.

Number 99-3-1, page 7, shows a nightdress sachet, which is made as follows: Take a piece of white linen damask 26 inches long by 17 inches wide, and from this cut a 10½-inch length for the front of the sachet, leaving a 15½-inch length to form the back and to turn over the flap. After the design is stamped upon the front and flap, proceed to work the passion-flowers, the petals in raised satin-stitch, the "rays" in bullion-stitch, and the rest of the flowers in satin-stitch, back-stitch, and French knots, as shown in the illustration. The round-petaled flowers are thickly padded and worked in French knots, and the centre is filled in with a circle of small buttonhole-stitches. Some of the leaves are embroidered with an outline of French knots, and filled with brier or coral-stitch worked to the shape; others are outlined with French knots, and veined with outline-stitch and bullion-stitch, while others are buttonholed in outline and filled in with one central line of French knots up each segment of the leaf; others, again, are worked in feather-stitch, the twist of the stitch itself forming a line of veining down the centre of the leaf. The ears of wheat are worked in double bullion-stitch (see Fig. 19), with a long stitch added on the point of each ear. The

FIG. 36. KNITTED FRINGE

stems are in outline-stitch and cording-stitch, and the tendrils are snail-stitch. When the embroidery is finished, the front piece of the sachet is turned down in a narrow hem where the sachet opens. Then the material is buttonholed together in scallops and the same buttonholing carried round the flap, as shown in the illustration, and a straight line of indented buttonholing (Fig. 14) is worked along the fold at the top of the flap. Cut away the material from the outside of the scallops and trim the sachet with fringe knitted according to the directions given above.

No. 99-3-3. POMEGRANATE FOR POWDERING
Perforated pattern, 4 x 3½ inches, 10 cents

NO. 611. MOUNTMELLICK CENTREPIECE.— Perforated pattern, 21 x 21 inches, cents. Stamped on white satin jean, cents. Mountmellick cotton for working, cents additional.

NO. 612. MOUNTMELLICK CENTREPIECE.— Perforated pattern, 20 x 20 inches, cents. Stamped on white satin jean, cents. Mountmellick cotton for working, cents additional.

NO. 99-3-1. NIGHTDRESS CASE IN MOUNTMELLICK EMBROIDERY— Perforated pattern, 16½ x 10½ inches, cents. Stamped on white satin jean, cents. Mountmellick cotton for working, additional.

No. 99-3-2. MOUNTMELLICK DOILY.—Perforated pattern, 11 x 11 inches, cents. Stamped on white satin jean, cents. Cotton for working, cents additional.

No. 510. DOILY.—Perforated pattern, 9½ x 13 inches, cents. Stamped on linen damask or jean, cents. Cotton for working, cents additional.

No. 602. MOUNTMELLICK TABLE COVER.—Perforated pattern, 16 x 16 inches, cents. Stamped on white satin jean, 36 x 36 inches, cents. Cotton for working four corners, additional.

No. 02-10-10. CENTREPIECE IN MOUNTMELLICK WORK.—Perforated pattern, 21 x 21 inches, cents. Stamped on white satin jean, cents. Mountmellick cotton for working, cents additional.

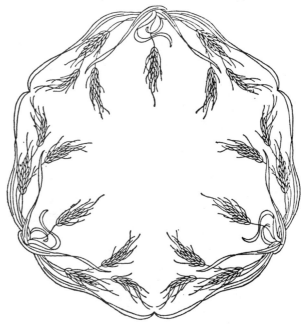

No. 00-10-18. CENTREPIECE IN MOUNTMELLICK WORK.—Perforated pattern, 19 x 19 inches, cents. Stamped on white satin jean, cents. Cotton for working, cents.

No. 02-12-9. WHEAT CENTREPIECE.—Perforated pattern, 20 x 20 inches, cents. Stamped on white satin jean, cents. White cotton for working, cents additional.

No. 99-8-14. Border for Mountmellick Work. — Perforated repeating pattern, 3 inches wide, cents.

No. 99-8-15. Alphabet for Mountmellick Embroidery.— Perforated pattern of Alphabet, 1⅝ inches high, cents.

No. 02-12-10. Grape Centrepiece. — Perforated pattern, 22½ x 22½ inches, cents. Stamped on linen, cents. White cotton for working, cents additional.

No. 03-6-9. Acorn Centrepiece. — Perforated pattern, 21 x 21 inches, cents. Stamped on white satin jean, cents. Mountmellick cotton for working, cents additional.

No. 03-2-12. Mountmellick Centrepiece. — Perforated pattern, 24 x 24 inches, cents. Stamped on white satin jean, cents. White cotton in two sizes for working, cents additional.

No. 03-6-6. Grape Centrepiece. — Perforated pattern, 25 x 25 inches, cents. Stamped on white satin jean, cents. Mountmellick cotton for working, cents additional.

No. 99-3-5. BOR-
DER FOR MOUNT-
MELLICK WORK. —
Perforated repeat-
ing pattern with cor-
ner, 3 inches wide,
cents.

No. 99-5-6. CORNER FOR MOUNTMEL-
LICK WORK. — Perforated pattern, 11½ x
11½ inches, cents. Stamped on linen
damask or jean, 36 inches square, cents,
Cotton for working four corners, cents.

No. 02-10-9. BABY'S BIB IN
MOUNTMELLICK WORK. — Perforated pattern, 10 x 12 inches, cents.
Stamped on white satin jean,
cents. Mountmellick cotton for
working, cents additional.

No. 99-3-6. BOR-
DER FOR MOUNT-
MELLICK WORK. —
Perforated repeat-
ing pattern with cor-
ner, 3½ inches wide,
cents.

No. 509. TRAY CLOTH. — Perforated pattern, 15 x 23
inches, cents. Stamped on hemstitched linen, 18 x 27,
cents. Cotton for working, cents.

No. 03-S-5. MOUNTMELLICK DESIGN FOR CORNERS OF LUNCH
CLOTHS OR CENTREPIECE. — Perforated pattern, 12 x 12 inches,
cents. Stamped on 36-inch hemstitched white linen lunch cloth,
Stamped on 36-inch square of white satin jean, cents. Mountmellick cotton for working four corners, cents additional.

No. 03-9-17. CORNER IN MOUNTMELLICK
WORK. — Perforated pattern, 8 x 11 inches,
cents. Stamped on 36-inch square of white
satin jean, cents. Stamped on 36-inch hemstitched white linen lunch cloth, Mountmellick cotton for working, cents additional.

No. 99-8-10. DOILY.—Perforated pattern, 8 x 8 inches, cents. Stamped on damask or jean, cents. Cotton for working, cents.

No. 99-8-11. DOILY.—Perforated pattern, 12½ x 9½ inches, cents. Stamped on damask or jean, cents. Cotton for working, cents.

No. 00-11-40. CORNER FOR MOUNTMELLICK WORK.—Perforated pattern, 11 x 11 inches, cents. Stamped on white satin jean, 36 x 36 inches, cents. Cotton for working four corners, cents.

No. 00-2-12. MOUNTMELLICK CUTWORK FOR BUREAU SCARF.—Perforated pattern, 14 x 9 inches, cents. Stamped on linen damask or jean, 45 x 18 inches, cents. Cotton for working two ends, cents.

No. 613. MOUNTMELLICK CENTREPIECE.—Perforated pattern, 24 x 24 inches, cents. Stamped on white satin jean, cents. Mountmellick cotton for working, cents additional.

No. 99-9-2. MOUNTMELLICK COVER FOR SOFA PILLOW.—Perforated pattern, 20 x 20 inches, cents. Stamped on cream ticking, cents. Cotton for working, cents additional.

No. 508. TRAY CLOTH.—Perforated pattern, 15 x 19 inches, cents. Stamped on white satin jean, cents. Cotton for working, cents.